How To Build A Strong Family

Dr. Adebo Tomomewo

How To Build A Strong Family
Dr. Adebo Tomomewo

ISBN: 978-1-908845-10-8

Published by
Golden Truth Publishing
Bwerick, Canada
www.goldentruth.pro
for
Anaktisi Publishing House,
London, UK

All Scripture quotations are taken from New International Version (NIV) Bible.

All rights reserved. No part of this publication may be reproduced, stored in a retrieval system, or transmitted in any from or by any means, mechanical, electronic, photocopying or otherwise without the prior written consent of the copyright owner.

Interior design by Igor Kotelnykov

Printed in the United Kingdom

Copyright © 2024 by Dr. Adebo Tomomewo

Table Of Contents

Chapter 1

The Foundation of a Strong Family 7
    Introduction: Embracing Wisdom 7
    Building a Wise and Strong Family 8
    The Journey to Wisdom 9

Chapter 2

Building a Strong Family Like David 10
    Introduction to David's Strength 10
    The Growth of a Strong Family 10
    Choosing a Partner with Discernment 11
    The Importance of Spiritual Background 12
    Securing Wisdom and Guidance 12
    Identifying and Overcoming Family Challenges 13
    The Wisdom and Strength of a Family 15

Chapter 3

Behind a Strong Family is a Strong Man 17
    The Role of the Spiritual Leader in the Family 18
    Building with God 18
    The Essence of a Strong Leader 19
    Spiritual State and Family Strength 19

Chapter 4

How to Make Yourself Strong in a Weak Family 22

Chapter 5

How to Know the Kind of Family You Are Marrying Into 28

Chapter 6

How to be Free from Demonic Family Patterns 32

Chapter 7

How David Became a Stronger House than Saul 35
    Personal Relationship with God and Devotion to His Kingdom 35
    David's wise attitude prevailed over Saul 38
    Wise behaviour and Attitude go hand in hand 44

Chapter 8

Symptoms of a House with Weak Family Bonds 46
- Spirit of Division 46
- Disunity 47
- Lack of Personal Intimacy with God 49

Chapter 9

Characteristics of a Strong Family 50
- 1. A Praying Family 50
- 2. Walking in Agreement 51
- 3. Blocking the Spirit of Division 53
- Overcoming Weak Family Patterns 53

Chapter 10

Wisdom for Building a Strong Family 55
- Understanding Wisdom in the Family Context 55
- Biblical Perspective on Wisdom 56
- Accessing Wisdom to Build a Strong Family 57
- Wisdom in Action: The Example of Daniel 58

Chapter 11

What Are The Different Dimensions Of Wisdom 60
- Dimension 1. Light 64
- Dimension 2. Knowledge 67
- Dimension 3. Understanding 70
- Dimension 4. Wisdom 72
- Dimensions 5. Spirit of Mastery 75
- Dimension 6. Supernatural Wisdom of God 76
- Dimension 7. Spirit of Excellence 77
- Dimension 8. Interpretation of Dreams 87
- Dimension 9. Showing of Hard Sentences 89
- Dimension 10. Dissolving of Doubt 92

Chapter 12

Twenty-One Facts About Wisdom for Building a Strong Family 94

How To Build A Strong Family

Chapter 1

The Foundation of a Strong Family

Introduction: Embracing Wisdom

The principal key for building a strong family is **Wisdom**. Therefore, if you want to build a strong family, you must apply your heart to wisdom. To be a strong man is not a function of muscular strength but wisdom. Hence, the Bible affirms that a wise man is strong:

> *Through wisdom is a house builded; and by understanding it is established: A wise man is a strong (man)*
>
> *Proverbs 24:3 (KJV)*

Wisdom is the principal spiritual force or ingredient that makes a strong family. Every strong family is built by wisdom. Thus, it's through the instrumentality of wisdom that a strong family is built:

PROVERBS 24:3 (KJV)

Building a Wise and Strong Family

You can build a strong family in a perverse world if you embrace Wisdom. A wise family is a strong family because wisdom is the principal ingredient that makes a strong family. So, you must be in possession of wisdom if you desire a strong family. Most family problems are wisdom problems, which is why you must pursue the wisdom that is from above to manage your affairs on the earth. Therefore, when you want to start a family, the first thing you must possess is wisdom. Similarly, God brought wisdom forth as the first of his works:

> *The LORD possessed me in the beginning of his way, Before his works of old.*
>
> PROVERBS 8:22 (KJV)

If you lack wisdom, you will also lack the capacity to build a strong family. I believe the reason you are reading this book is that you have the desire to learn how to build a durable and strong family, in this 21st century where many are building disposable families.

The Journey to Wisdom

The journey to wisdom begins with **Knowledge**, which is information acquisition, while **Understanding** is the comprehension of the knowledge you have acquired, and **Wisdom** is the application of the knowledge comprehended. I'm excited you are reading this book to get knowledge and understand that led ultimately to wisdom.

If things are not going the way you desire, it means there is something you don't know; a gap in knowledge. I believe that gap is what you want to fill by reading this book. I pray that you will become wiser as you read this book.

Chapter 2

Building a Strong Family Like David

Introduction to David's Strength

> *Now there was long war between the house of Saul and the house of David: but David waxed stronger and stronger, and the house of Saul waxed weaker and weaker.*
>
> **2 Samuel 3:1 KJV**

The Growth of a Strong Family

Why was David's family a stronger family? It was because David was warring with wisdom, making it difficult for Saul to defeat him. Through observation, we notice that David waxed stronger as he defended the generation of the house of David. This was due to his wisdom and strong relationship with God as detailed in 1 Samuel 18:5,14-15,30.

5 And David went out whithersoever Saul sent him, and behaved himself wisely: and Saul set him over the men of war, and he was accepted in the sight of all the people, and also in the sight of Saul's servants.

14 And David behaved himself wisely in all his ways; and the Lord was with him.

15 Wherefore when Saul saw that he behaved himself very wisely, he was afraid of him.

30 Then the princes of the Philistines went forth: and it came to pass, after they went forth, that David behaved himself more wisely than all the servants of Saul; so that his name was much set by.

1 SAMUEL 18:5,14-15,30

Proverbs 24:3-5 tells us, "A wise man is strong," indicating that the wiser you are, the stronger you become, as you wage your war with wise counsel. We should seek the wisdom to make our families strong in the name of our Lord Jesus.

Choosing a Partner with Discernment

When choosing a partner, it's essential to discern the kind of family you are marrying into. Every family is either a house of David (strong family) or the house of Saul (weak family). In the realms of the spirit, each family is a house; you are either marrying into a strong or a weak family spiritually.

For example, choosing a partner from the house of Saul means marrying into a potentially weak family. As **Proverbs 18:14 AMPC** states, "The strong spirit of a man sustains him in bodily pain or trouble, but a weak and broken spirit who can raise up or bear?"

The Importance of Spiritual Background

Success in a relationship often depends on coming from a strong spiritual background and having a personal relationship with God. A weak or broken family can be identified by the characteristics and life events of its members. This is why intense prayer and seeking God's guidance is crucial before marriage.

Securing Wisdom and Guidance

Before taking any crucial step in life, such as marriage, it's vital to secure wisdom first, as indicated in **Proverbs 8:22**.

> *The Lord possessed me in the beginning of his way, before his works of old.*
>
> PROVERBS 8:22.

Pray to the Holy Spirit, our counselor, for direction. The Bible refers to Him as the spirit of wisdom, helping us to see beyond mere appearances, as shown in **Job 28:9.** "Wisdom is profitable to direct," says **Ecclesiastes 10:10**. Following the directions of the Holy Spirit can help overcome challenges, as God's guidance is secured from the beginning, illustrated in **Genesis 1:1-3**.

> *In the beginning God created the heaven and the earth. And the earth was without form, and void; and darkness was upon the face of the deep. And the Spirit of God moved upon the face of the waters. And God said, Let there be light: and there was light.*
>
> GENESIS 1:1-3

Identifying and Overcoming Family Challenges

It's important to be aware of the signs of a weak martial family, such as prevalent divorce or struggles with health and fertility. These indicators can prepare you to handle foundational issues in your relationships. **Matthew 22:23-27** provides an example of collective captivity in a family, where all men died in the same marriage.

> *The same day came to him the Sadducees, which say that there is no resurrection, and asked him, Saying, Master, Moses said, If a man die, having no children, his brother shall marry his wife, and raise up seed unto his brother. Now there were with us seven brethren: and the first, when he had married a wife, deceased, and, having no issue, left his wife unto his brother: Likewise the second also, and the third, unto the seventh. And last of all the woman died also.*
>
> MATTHEW 22:23-27

To build a strong family, establish a strong relationship with the Lord. Challenges will arise, but strength in the Lord and the power of His might through prayers will lead to victory.

> *Finally, my brethren, be strong in the Lord, and in the power of his might. Put on the whole armour*

> *of God, that ye may be able to stand against the wiles of the devil.*
>
> *EPHESIANS 6:10-11 KJV*

A strong family is a winning family, overcoming life's battles. May any force against the positive prophecy of your family be scattered in Jesus' name.

Psalms 115:10 promises that God will bless and increase our families.

> *O house of Aaron, trust in the Lord: he is their help and their shield.*
>
> *PSALMS 115:10*

The Wisdom and Strength of a Family

Read and reinforce your family by the word of God. Remember, as **Matthew 16:18** says, "I will build my church, and the gates of hell shall not prevail," and it is through wisdom that a house is built. A wise family is a strong family. Your strength is in your wisdom.

A strong family has a robust spiritual immune system. As stated in **Proverbs 18:14**, it is the strong spirit that sustains you in times of trouble. The real you is your spirit; therefore, the sequence should be spirit, soul, and body, with a developed strong spirit leading the soul and body.

And the very God of peace sanctify you wholly; and I pray God your whole spirit and soul and body be preserved blameless unto the coming of our Lord Jesus Christ.

1 Thessalonians 5:23 KJV

Wisdom strengthens your spirit, and its absence leads to weakness, potentially resulting in a weak family. It takes wisdom to build a strong spirit and, in turn, a strong family.

CHAPTER 3

Behind a Strong Family is a Strong Man

Now there was long war between the house of Saul and the house of David: but David waxed stronger and stronger, and the house of Saul waxed weaker and weaker.

2 SAMUEL *3:1 KJV*

David, despite being the last born of Jesse's eight children, carried his family's spiritual lineage. His position in the family was not as pivotal as his strong position in God. David took responsibility for his family's spiritual welfare, understanding that a family's strength is a reflection of its spiritual fortitude.

> *...But David waxed stronger...*

The Role of the Spiritual Leader in the Family

The strength of David was a cornerstone for his family. If David had been weak, the entire family would have followed suit. It illustrates that every strong family is anchored by a spiritually strong individual. Building a strong relationship with God through daily study of the word and maintaining a robust personal prayer life are essential. Praying for each family member by name, as exemplified by the Apostle Paul, is crucial.

> *Cease not to give thanks for you, making mention of you in my prayers;*
>
> EPHESIANS *1:16 KJV*

This commitment in prayer is one of the key ways a spiritual leader strengthens their household. As you grow in prayer, your family, much like the house of David, grows in strength.

Building with God

> *Except the LORD build the house, They labour in vain that build it: Except the LORD keep the city, The watchman waketh but in vain.*
>
> PSALM *127:1 KJV*

Partnering with God in building your family ensures His protection and guidance. Without God as the watchman, efforts can be futile. A strong family requires intentional effort, not just happenstance.

> *For every house is builded by some man; but he that built all things is God.*
>
> HEBREWS *3:4 KJV*

The Essence of a Strong Leader

Behind every strong family stands a man, in partnership with God, the ultimate builder. This partnership extends to all aspects of life, be it family, church, business, or career. David's strength allowed his family to prevail against Saul, demonstrating the necessity of enduring strength in life's battles. The ability to face and overcome challenges is a hallmark of a strong individual.

Spiritual State and Family Strength

> *But ye, beloved, building up yourselves on your most holy faith, praying in the Holy Ghost,*
>
> JUDE *1:20 KJV*

Your spiritual state directly influences your family. Being prayerful and spiritually strong can have a positive impact on your family, especially in times of struggle.

Your actions, whether good or bad, impact your family. Private wrongdoings and embracing wicked ways will negatively affect your family, as illustrated in Exodus 20:4-5.

> *Thou shalt not make unto thee any graven image, or any likeness of any thing that is in heaven above, or that is in the earth beneath, or that is in the water under the earth. Thou shalt not bow down thyself to them, nor serve them: for I the Lord thy God am a jealous God, visiting the iniquity of the fathers upon the children unto the third and fourth generation of them that hate me;*
>
> Exodus 20:4-5

The contrasting examples of David and Saul highlight the importance of being strong in the Lord and the power of His might for the sake of your family's destiny.

> *Finally, my brethren, be strong in the Lord, and in the power of his might.*
>
> Ephesians *6:10*

God seeks individuals with a heart for Him, reminiscent of David. The strength of your family hinges on your personal pursuit of God. Your daily interactions with God will inevitably influence your immediate family, emphasizing the importance of being fervent and passionate in your spiritual journey.

In conclusion, the strength and stability of a family are deeply connected to the spiritual leadership provided by its members. It calls for a deliberate and consistent effort to grow in faith and maintain a close relationship with God, impacting not only personal destiny but also the destiny of the entire family.

CHAPTER 4

How to Make Yourself Strong in a Weak Family

And it came to pass, while there was war between the house of Saul and the house of David, that Abner made himself strong for the house of Saul.

2 SAMUEL 3:6 KJV

Consider the scripture above: you can make yourself strong, even if you come from a weak family - like the house of Saul - by connecting with those from a strong family, as Abner did by connecting with David.

And Abner sent messengers to David on his behalf, saying, Whose is the land? saying also, Make thy league with me, and, behold, my hand shall be with thee, to bring about all Israel unto thee. And he said, Well; I will make a league with thee: but one thing I require of thee, that

> *is, Thou shalt not see my face, except thou first bring Michal Saul's daughter, when thou comest to see my face.*
>
> 2 Samuel *3:12-13 KJV*

This passage is an exemplary instance of someone from a weak family (House of Saul) forming an alliance with someone from a strong family (House of David). The Holy Spirit guides someone from a strong family to forge a relationship with someone from a weak family, thereby offsetting that family's frailty and creating a new paradigm. What you don't receive by revelation, you can gain through relationship. This principle applies not only to marriage but also to business partnerships, ministry, and career pursuits. Seek out the "house of David," look for strong men and women — God Chasers — passionate for the things of God. Shun bad company, avoid a sinful lifestyle, and do not live in a manner displeasing to God. Align with the Davids of this generation.

Do not, from a spiritually weak "house of Saul," choose a partner from another weak house, compounding frailty upon frailty. The wise man knows:

> *He that walketh with wise men shall be wise: But a companion of fools shall be destroyed.*
>
> Proverbs *13:20 KJV*

Abner demonstrated wisdom by allying with David to fulfill God's will for Israel. If you surround yourself with four wise individuals, you will soon be the fifth. This principle holds true for foolishness as well. Being wise means associating with spiritually robust individuals.

The Bible instructs believers to be strong in the Lord through our intimate union with Him, drawing on the power of His might—referring to the Holy Spirit. The Amplified Bible articulates it thus:

> ...be strong in the Lord [be empowered through your union with Him]; draw your strength from Him [that strength which His boundless might provides]. Put on God's whole armor [the armor of a heavy-armed soldier which God supplies], that you may be able successfully to stand up against [all] the strategies and the deceits of the devil. For we are not wrestling with flesh and blood [contending only with physical opponents], but against the despotisms, against the powers, against [the master spirits who are] the world rulers of this present darkness, against the spirit forces of wickedness in the heavenly (supernatural) sphere. Therefore put on God's complete armor, that you may be able to resist and stand your ground on the evil day [of danger], and,

> *having done all [the crisis demands], to stand [firmly in your place].*
>
> *EPHESIANS 6:10-13 AMPC*

Without strength in the Lord, one cannot win the spiritual battles or overcome the negative patterns maintained by the "strong man" in some families. Like Gideon, you must be robust in the Lord and in the might of the Holy Spirit to vanquish the ancestral forces of your lineage. A strong family that cooperates with God will triumph in life's battles.

I pray that every force opposing positive prophecy in your family is scattered in the name of the Lord Jesus. Remember:

> *O house of Aaron, trust in the LORD: He is their help and their shield.*
>
> *PSALM 115:10 KJV*

God will bless and increase us and our children in health and peace. We are here to affirm the Word of God over our families, and as Matthew 16:18 declares, through wisdom a house is built.

And I say also unto thee, That thou art Peter, and upon this rock I will build my church; and the gates of hell shall not prevail against it.

Matthew 16:18 KJV

A wise family is a strong family; the more wisdom you possess, the stronger you become. Your strength lies in your wisdom. Build a strong spiritual immune system, for a robust spirit will sustain you in times of trouble. Your life's engine is your spirit, and wisdom is the fortifier of your spirit.

A weak family is prone to fracture, but wisdom can fortify you. Pursue knowledge as Proverbs suggests:

A wise man is strong; yea, a man of knowledge increaseth strength.

Proverbs 24:5 KJV

The spiritual man within you, like a child, needs to grow to spiritual maturity. This requires time to build into a durable and stronger spiritual presence, and exposure to knowledge is key. Nourish your spirit with books, anointed messages, Bible School, and regular church attendance. You are what you consume—wisdom strengthens you, making you wiser and more formidable than your adversaries.

O how love I thy law! It is my meditation all the day. Thou through thy commandments hast made me wiser than mine enemies: For they are ever with me.

Psalms 119:97-98 KJV

Knowledge is the vehicle that transforms weakness into strength, and as you progress from one level of understanding to the next, you grow stronger.

The Bible warns:

If thou faint in the day of adversity, thy strength is small.

Proverbs 24:10 KJV

A faint heart is a symptom of inadequate strength, but a heart can become robust through knowledge. The scripture in Daniel reinforces this truth:

And such as do wickedly against the covenant shall he corrupt by flatteries: but the people that do know their God shall be strong, and do exploits.

Daniel 11:32 KJV

Your pursuit of knowledge in any aspect of life amplifies your strength in that area. Therefore, seek knowledge to turn your weaknesses into strengths.

Chapter 5

How to Know the Kind of Family You Are Marrying Into

Understanding the family you are marrying into or have married into now is crucial. By inquiring about the pattern of events or occurrences in that family, you can discern its nature. Consider the marital status of its members. Are they predominantly married, divorced, or single parents? Patterns of martial weakness may be evident in families where divorce is common or where single parenthood is frequent.

If you are entering a marital relationship with someone from such a family, be aware that you might face significant challenges in overcoming these negative marital patterns. Should problems arise in your marital journey, the advice you receive from a spouse who comes from a family with a history of divorce might not be conducive to sustaining your marriage. However, if you apply the principles of durable marriage as taught in the Word of God and approach them prayerfully, you can overcome these challenges. Remember, prevailing over negative family patterns is possible through faith.

In contrast, marrying into a family where siblings are happily married and have built strong homes is a sign of a robust family unit. This is why I advise single individuals not to marry blindly, as Jacob did with Leah. Do not marry in darkness; marry in the light and understanding of the Word of God. Ask questions, understand the family's rules for marriage, and learn from the example of Laban's deception of Jacob in the Bible:

> *And it came to pass, that in the morning, behold, it was Leah: and he said to Laban, What is this thou hast done unto me? did not I serve with thee for Rachel? wherefore then hast thou beguiled me? And Laban said, It must not be so done in our country, to give the younger before the firstborn. Fulfil her week, and we will give thee this also for the service which thou shalt serve with me yet seven other years.*
>
> *GENESIS* **29:25-27 KJV**

Rushing into marriage without proper knowledge and research can lead to regret. A broken courtship is preferable to a broken marriage. Use the courtship period to discern whether you are marrying into the house of Saul or the house of David. This discernment is a golden rule before saying 'I do.'

Also, consider the health history of the family. Some families struggle with hereditary diseases like cancer or mental health issues. Such information is vital, just as life insurance companies inquire about family health history.

In the Bible, there is an example of a family pattern leading to collective captivity:

> *The same day came to him the Sadducees, which say that there is no resurrection, and asked him, saying, Master, Moses said, If a man die, having no children, his brother shall marry his wife, and raise up seed unto his brother. Now there were with us seven brethren: and the first, when he had married a wife, deceased, and, having no issue, left his wife unto his brother: And last of all the woman died also. Therefore in the resurrection whose wife shall she be of the seven? for they all had her. Jesus answered and said unto them, Ye do err, not knowing the scriptures, nor the power of God. For in the resurrection they neither marry, nor are given in marriage, but are as the angels of God in heaven.*
>
> MATTHEW 22:23-25, 27-30 KJV

Such patterns are strongholds against the knowledge of God and must be confronted with spiritual warfare:

> *For though we walk in the flesh, we do not war after the flesh: (for the weapons of our warfare are not carnal, but mighty through God to the pulling down of strong holds;) casting down imaginations, and every high thing that exalteth itself against the knowledge of God, and bringing into captivity every thought to the obedience of Christ; and having in a readiness to revenge all disobedience, when your obedience is fulfilled.*
>
> *2 Corinthians 10:3-6 KJV*

In summary, discerning the nature of the family you are marrying into is crucial. Seek guidance from the Holy Spirit and do not be driven by lust, as this can lead to being lost in marriage. Be vigilant against negative family patterns and seek God's wisdom and strength to overcome them.

Chapter 6

How to be Free from Demonic Family Patterns

The devil often conceals his true identity behind various situations, people, and circumstances. If you observe a consistent pattern, such as significant delays in your marital life or relationships that end for very trivial reasons, it's important to recognize this as a potential spiritual issue. When such occurrences repeat themselves - once, twice, thrice - it signifies a pattern. This pattern likely points to the influence of a spiritual entity, known as the strongman, responsible for these trends.

As believers, we must be vigilant, for Satan constantly seeks to render us unfruitful. When he finds a believer in a lukewarm state, he attempts to master and influence them, seeking to establish his territory in their life. Over time, you might notice a logical and scientific pattern in your life, indicating the presence of an intelligent entity - the strongman - masquerading behind these circumstances to bring you into bondage.

It is important to understand that such spirits often reveal themselves in dreams. When under the influence of a spirit, it is nearly impossible not to encounter them in your dreams. Similarly, walking with the Holy Ghost brings dreams, intelligence, and revelation, whether or not you are naturally inclined to dream. He will manifest in your dreams to assure you of His presence. As stated in Joel 2:28-29, 32 (KJV):

> *And it shall come to pass afterward, that I will pour out my spirit upon all flesh; and your sons and your daughters shall prophesy, your old men shall dream dreams, your young men shall see visions: and also upon the servants and upon the handmaids in those days will I pour out my spirit.*
>
> *And it shall come to pass, that whosoever shall call on the name of the LORD shall be delivered: for in mount Zion and in Jerusalem shall be deliverance, as the LORD hath said, and in the remnant whom the LORD shall call.*
>
> *JOEL 2:28-29, 32 (KJV)*

Engagement with spirits often leads to seeing their imagery because when they pass through your space, they activate your soul and manifest through images, thoughts, and pictures - the general language of spirits. If you experience repetitive dreams, recurring thoughts, or see demonic images, it is a strong indication of a spiritual entity influencing your life.

To break the strongman's influence, prayer is essential. Understanding the nature of these spirits and how to pray effectively against them is crucial to stop their activities in your life. As you apply the principles revealed in this chapter, you may experience various symptoms, but it's vital to stay the course and not be deterred by fear. This chapter aims to empower those engaged in spiritual warfare, providing insights into recognizing and overcoming demonic entities responsible for patterns, dreams, thoughts, and images that negatively impact your life and family.

Chapter 7

How David Became a Stronger House than Saul

Personal Relationship with God and Devotion to His Kingdom

David was a man after God's heart and a lover of God the Father. He passionately pursued intimacy with God, seeking to know the Lord. David was a true God chaser, and such individuals grow strong by drawing their strength from their union with the Lord. This truth is encapsulated in the Biblical verse:

> *And such as do wickedly against the covenant shall he corrupt by flatteries: but the people that do know their God shall be strong, and do exploits.*
>
> Daniel **11:32 KJV**

The deeper our knowledge of God, the stronger we become spiritually. This is affirmed in Proverbs 24:5, stating that "a man of knowledge increases strength." David's complete devotion to God and His earthly purpose, coupled with his leadership philosophy rooted in the fear of God, starkly contrasts with Saul's lack of such an intimate relationship with the Lord.

> *Now these be the last words of David. David the son of Jesse said, And the man who was raised up on high, The anointed of the God of Jacob, And the sweet psalmist of Israel, said, The Spirit of the LORD spake by me, And his word was in my tongue. The God of Israel said, The Rock of Israel spake to me, He that ruleth over men must be just, Ruling in the fear of God.*
>
> 2 Samuel 23:1-3 KJV

The fear of God is fundamental to the security of any marital relationship. Its absence can lead to transgressions such as adultery and fornication. Joseph's destiny was secured by his fear of God, and similarly, our standing before God is measured by the state of our hearts.

> *There is none greater in this house than I; neither hath he kept back any thing from me but thee,*

> *because thou art his wife: how then can I do this great wickedness, and sin against God?*
>
> GENESIS **39:9**

God shows His strength on behalf of those whose hearts are wholly devoted to Him.

> *For the eyes of the LORD run to and fro throughout the whole earth, to shew himself strong in the behalf of them whose heart is perfect toward him. Herein thou hast done foolishly: therefore from henceforth thou shalt have wars.*
>
> 2 CHRONICLES **16:9 KJV**

At the heart of the matter is the matter of the heart. The Bible calls David "a man after God's heart," which is the key reason David grew stronger and stronger while the house of Saul became weaker. Saul's waning relationship with God (1 Samuel 3:1) further exemplifies this contrast.

> *And when he had removed him, he raised up unto them David to be their king; to whom also he gave testimony, and said, I have found David the son of Jesse, a man after mine own heart, which shall fulfil all my will.*
>
> ACTS **13:22 KJV**

David's wise attitude prevailed over Saul

David became stronger and stronger because David was warring with wisdom.

> *And David behaved himself wisely in all his ways; and the LORD was with him. Wherefore when Saul saw that he behaved himself very wisely, he was afraid of him.*
>
> 1 SAMUEL *18:14-15 KJV*

David representing the house of David became stronger than Saul's. His house became of wise attribute in all his ways. If you possess wisdom it will manifest in your behaviour, this is a major areas many people don't give attention to, "your behaviour".

You are either behaving wisely or foolishly. Wise behavior is one of evidence of someone that is strong spirit in God, strong men wisdom made.

Hence, foolish behaviour is evidence someone operating from a weak spirit.

Show me a man that is well behaved, I will show you a wise man, he is able to control his attitude.

One of the way you know a foolish person or a wise person is when they open their mouth.

Wise behaviour is what we call character and integrity today,

So many people are behaving like those from the house of Saul with foolishness as evidence today, It good to noted that it was foolishness that destroyed the throne of Saul

> *And Samuel said to Saul, Thou hast done foolishly: thou hast not kept the commandment of the LORD thy God, which he commanded thee: for now would the LORD have established thy kingdom upon Israel for ever. But now thy kingdom shall not continue: the LORD hath sought him a man after his own heart, and the LORD hath commanded him to be captain over his people, because thou hast not kept that which the LORD commanded thee.*
>
> 1 SAMUEL 13:13-14 KJV

You can see from the above bible verses you can see the effect of Saul foolishness which one of the forces that made his family house a weak house, when you see individuals or people from a weak house you see foolishness on display and on the other hand it was through wisdom that the house of David took over leadership from the house of Saul.

Also you have learnt that a lot of David wise behaviour is rooted in the fear of God

And unto man he said, Behold, the fear of the Lord, that is wisdom; And to depart from evil is understanding.

Job 28:28 KJV

David had opportunity to kill Saul on his journey to become the king he never touched him even though Saul was out to kill him.

Fear of God is one of Ingredients of a strong family that open the door of wisdom to him.

9 Instruct the wise and they will be wiser still; teach the righteous and they will add to their learning. 10 The fear of the LORD is the beginning of wisdom, and knowledge of the Holy One is understanding. 11 For through wisdom your days will be many, and years will be added to your life.

Proverbs 9:10 (NIV)

So, a family that fear God will attract the flow of wisdom like the house of Cornelius in Acts10:1-4

At Caesarea there was a man named Cornelius, a centurion in what was known as the Italian Regiment. He and all his family were devout and God-fearing; he gave generously to those in need and prayed to God regularly. One day at about three in the afternoon he had a vision. He distinctly saw an angel of God, who came to him and said, "Cornelius!" Cornelius stared at him in fear. "What is it, Lord?" he asked. The angel answered, "Your prayers and gifts to the poor have come up as a memorial offering before God.

Acts 10:1-4 (NIV)

This is why the house of Saul was weak, he lacked the fear of God and lacked the wisdom of God. Unlike Saul, David's heart was sensitive to the nudging and restraint of the Holy Spirit not to shed blood while the insensitivity heart of Saul and his conscience was completely dead. How sensitive is our heart to the restraint of the Holy Spirit? Is the This is what determines the level of power you manifest on the earth. So how strong you are on the earth realms is tied to the level of your connectivity to the Holy Spirit nudging.

And the men of David said unto him, Behold the day of which the LORD said unto thee, Behold, I will deliver thine enemy into thine hand, that thou mayest do to him as it shall seem good unto thee. Then David arose, and cut off the skirt of Saul's robe privily. And it came to pass afterward, that David's heart smote him, because he had cut off Saul's skirt. And he said unto his men, The LORD forbid that I should do this thing unto my master, the LORD's anointed, to stretch forth mine hand against him, seeing he is the anointed of the LORD. So, David stayed his servants with these words, and suffered them not to rise against Saul. But Saul rose up out of the cave, and went on his way. David also arose afterward, and went out of the cave, and cried after Saul, saying, My Lord the king. And when Saul looked behind him, David stooped with his face to the earth, and bowed himself. And David said to Saul, wherefore hearest thou men's words, saying, Behold, David seeketh thy hurt?

Behold, this day thine eyes have seen how that the LORD had delivered thee to day into mine hand in the cave: and some bade me kill thee: but mine eye spared thee; and I said, I will not put forth mine hand against my Lord; for he is the LORD's anointed. As saith the proverb of the ancients, Wickedness proceedeth from the wicked: but mine hand shall not be upon thee. For if a man find his enemy, will he let him go well away? wherefore the LORD reward thee good for that thou hast done unto me this day. And now, behold, I know well that thou shalt surely be king, and that the kingdom of Israel shall be established in thine hand. Swear now therefore unto me by the LORD, that thou wilt not cut off my seed after me, and that thou wilt not destroy my name out of my father's house.

1 Samuel *24:4-10, 13, 19-21 KJV*

The wise behaviour of David is rooted in the fear of God, he had wisdom that nobody has to be dethroned for Him to be enthroned so when you are plotting to bring individuals that are of higher rank to you down so that you can move ahead or looking for how to destroy other people so you gain recognition for promotion with the Intension to take their position up, that its foolish behaviour that will come back to hurt and make you like the house of Saul, that is evidence you are operating under of a weak spirit. It is the spirit of cribs.

Make it your policy that no one must come down through your hands because he that digs a pit, will fall into it, it takes a strong spirit to cover up the errors of those ahead of you if you want to pull down someone ahead of you, the grace that took that person to that higher position will disgrace you, someone says what of those in the high office ahead that are doing wrong? Leave them for God to judge them himself.

You cannot build a strong family as a person without a Christ-like strong character in the foundation of your life.

Nevertheless, the foundation of God standeth sure, having this seal, The Lord knoweth them that are his. And, Let every one that nameth the name of Christ depart from iniquity. But in a great house there are not only vessels of gold and of silver, but also of wood and of earth; and

> *some to honour, and some to dishonour. If a man therefore purge himself from these, he shall be a vessel unto honour, sanctified, and meet for the master's use, and prepared unto every good work. Flee also youthful lusts: but follow righteousness, faith, charity, peace, with them that call on the Lord out of a pure heart.*
>
> *2 Timothy 2:19-22 KJV*

You can see from the Bible verse that your departure from iniquity will determine the kind of the destiny of your house and the quality of vessels that emerge from that house.

Also departure from iniquity is a sure foundation for any one that walk in strong character, this is reason a man of character will outlast a man of charisma. A wise man once said and I quote:

> *Worry about your character not your reputation, your character is who you are and your reputation is who people think you are*

Wise behaviour and Attitude go hand in hand

Our Behaviour has its roots in our attitudes as believers, that was what made a major difference between David and Saul.

What mark David out is his God centred attitude towards life and approach to people and things.

The definition of attitude is a settled way of thinking or feeling about someone or something, typically one that is reflected in a person's behavior.

Our outward behaviour and character are largely the manifestation of our inward attitudes, it's your attitude that determines your altitude in life, the difference between David's strong house of David' and Saul's weak house is attitude. Attitude is also the difference between a leader and a slave, put a man at the top that has a bad attitude like Saul in power, His attitude will change his level to a slave and similarly take someone like David in his low estate in the bush with a good attitude he would become a leader, your attitude is like a lift. Its either taking you up and bringing you down.

For instance, they imprisoned Joseph physically but they could not imprison his attitude, this is the reason he was in prison but he never became a prisoner, so what makes a man is it's the attitude on his inside.

Chapter 8

Symptoms of a House with Weak Family Bonds

Spirit of Division

"*United we stand, divided we fall.*" This timeless wisdom, resonating through **Genesis 13:8**, underscores the pernicious impact of division within a family. Strife, a subtle yet destructive force, can sever the strongest of familial ties. The biblical narrative of Abraham and Lot exemplifies this; only upon Lot's departure did Abraham's communion with God resume. Such division, often the machination of malevolent forces, aims to thwart a family's potential and progress. It is imperative, therefore, for the discerning and mature members of the family to confront and quell these divisions.

In every family, let there be an 'Abraham' - a beacon of maturity and wisdom, advocating for unity and reconciliation. Genesis chapter 14 illustrates this beautifully, where Abraham's mended relationship with Lot enables him to intercede on Lot's behalf in chapter 19. This act of peacemaking aligns with the biblical injunction in **1 Corinthians 14:20**: to be mature in understanding yet childlike in malice.

Matthew 5:9 further illuminates this principle: *"Blessed are the peacemakers: for they shall be called the children of God."* The role of a peacemaker extends beyond mere conflict resolution; it involves fostering a spirit of unity and understanding, even in the face of disagreement. Such peacemakers become instruments through which God can work, salvaging and strengthening the family unit.

Disunity

Psalms 133:1 poetically articulates the beauty of unity:

> *Behold, how good and how pleasant it is for brethren to dwell together in unity!*
>
> Psalms *133:1*

Unity breeds blessings and progress, while division leads to familial defeat. The story of the Tower of Babel in **Genesis 11:1-6** serves as a stark reminder of the consequences of disunity. When a community unites in purpose, they become formidable; division, however, sows the seeds of their downfall.

In a similar vein, **Proverbs 6:16-19** and **Matthew 12:25** highlight the destructive nature of division.

> *And Jesus knew their thoughts, and said unto them, Every kingdom divided against itself is brought to desolation; and every city or house divided against itself shall not stand*
>
> MATTHEW 12:25

A house divided against itself cannot stand, be it a family or a church. **Psalm 55:9** underscores this truth within the context of the church.

> *Destroy, O Lord, and divide their tongues: for I have seen violence and strife in the city.*
>
> PSALM 55:9

Division, often manifested in misunderstandings and misinterpretations, is a tool used by malevolent forces to dismantle the family structure. As in the Trinity, where the Father, Son, and Holy Spirit work in harmonious unity, families must strive to respect and love each other despite differing views.

Lack of Personal Intimacy with God

The biblical figure of Saul epitomizes the downfall that ensues from a severed relationship with God. As a monarch, Saul's earthly rule was inextricably linked to his spiritual communion with the divine. This principle holds true for family leaders as well; their stewardship and guidance are potentiated through a deep, personal relationship with God. A family's spiritual health is often a reflection of its members' intimacy with God. Therefore, nurturing this personal relationship is paramount for the overall strength and resilience of the family unit.

CHAPTER 9

Characteristics of a Strong Family

1. A Praying Family

The strength of a family often parallels the vigor of its prayer life. It's commonly said, "The family that prays together, stays together." Prayer is the channel through which weaknesses transform into strengths by the Holy Spirit's ministry.

The Bible affirms this in Romans 8:26 KJV:

> *Likewise the Spirit also helpeth our infirmities: for we know not what we should pray for as we ought: but the Spirit itself maketh intercession for us with groanings which cannot be uttered.*
>
> ROMANS *8:26 KJV*

Establishing personal prayer altars, your sacred communion with God, is crucial. David's strength was nurtured in his secret place with God. In contrast, Saul's lack of such a place led him astray to seek guidance from a sorcerer. Strengthen yourself, especially through praying in the Holy Spirit, as advised in Jude 1:20 KJV:

> *But ye, beloved, building up yourselves on your most holy faith, praying in the Holy Ghost.*
>
> *JUDE 1:20 KJV*

2. Walking in Agreement

> *To this one I will look [graciously], To him who is humble and contrite in spirit, and who [reverently] trembles at My word and honors My commands.*
>
> *ISAIAH 66:2 AMP*

In Deutcronomy 30:2, we are reminded of the power of unity. A family's agreement sets the stage for dominion, making it robust enough to overcome the devil's schemes.

> *And shalt return unto the Lord thy God, and shalt obey his voice according to all that I command thee this day, thou and thy children, with all thine heart, and with all thy soul;*
>
> *DEUTERONOMY 30:2*

This dominion is fostered by adhering to God's Word as the ultimate authority. When both partners align with God's Word, they position themselves for dominance. Disagreements often arise when either partner rejects the Word's correction, usually due to pride.

Isaiah 66:2 AMP highlights the value of humility:

> *...But to this one I will look [graciously], To him who is humble and contrite in spirit, and who [reverently] trembles at My word and honors My commands.*
>
> *ISAIAH 66:2 AMP*

Embracing God's Word with humility attracts His grace, as mentioned in James 4:6, strengthening the marital bond and shielding the family from disgrace and failure.

> *But he giveth more grace. Wherefore he saith, God resisteth the proud, but giveth grace unto the humble.*
>
> *JAMES 4:6*

3. Blocking the Spirit of Division

What therefore God hath joined together, let not man put asunder.
MATTHEW **19:6 KJV**

Understanding your spouse is key, seeing things from God's perspective. Misunderstandings can give the devil a foothold. Effective communication and nurturing sexual intimacy are vital, as is guarding against third-party interference in your marriage. The Biblical warning in Matthew 19:6 KJV underscores this: "Wherefore they are no more twain, but one flesh. What therefore God hath joined together, let not man put asunder." David's downfall due to his infidelity is a cautionary tale. However, his repentance and the subsequent strength he gained provide hope for overcoming familial challenges.

Overcoming Weak Family Patterns

Regardless of your family's current state, transformation is possible through spiritual responsibility. Like David, growing stronger in spirit confronts any demonic influence in your lineage. Luke 11:21-22 KJV illustrates this: "When a strong man armed keepeth his palace, his goods are in peace: but when a stronger than he shall come upon him, and overcome him, he taketh from him all his armour wherein he trusted, and divideth his spoils." Overcoming the 'strongman' in your family requires a firm spiritual stance. The continuous battle between the houses of Saul and David, as recounted in 2 Samuel 3:1 KJV, exemplifies the triumph of spiritual fortitude: "Now there was long war between the house of Saul and the house of David: but David waxed stronger and stronger, and the house of Saul waxed weaker and weaker." Strive to be a stronger believer, for victory in the spirit will fortify your family against any adversity.

Chapter 10

Wisdom for Building a Strong Family

Understanding Wisdom in the Family Context

Without a clear definition, there can be deviation. So, what exactly is wisdom in the context of building a strong family? Wisdom is the right use of knowledge. It is the grace to apply what you know effectively. It does not benefit one to possess knowledge if it is not applied correctly. There is an abundance of knowledge, but wisdom is the proper application of the knowledge we have acquired. Knowledge is the collection of information; understanding is the comprehension of this information; and wisdom is the application of this understanding, especially in the context of the Word of God.

Biblical Perspective on Wisdom

The Bible says:

> *Therefore whosoever heareth these sayings of mine, and doeth them, I will liken him unto a wise man, which built his house upon a rock: and the rain descended, and the floods came, and the winds blew, and beat upon that house; and it fell not: for it was founded upon a rock. And every one that heareth these sayings of mine, and doeth them not, shall be likened unto a foolish man, which built his house upon the sand: and the rain descended, and the floods came, and the winds blew, and beat upon that house; and it fell: and great was the fall of it.*
>
> MATTHEW 7:24-27 KJV

Wisdom in this context is building your family upon the Word of God, providing scriptural solutions to every family issue. In the book of Job, wisdom is further defined:

> *And unto man he said, Behold, the fear of the Lord, that is wisdom; And to depart from evil is understanding.*
>
> JOB 28:28 KJV

Accessing Wisdom to Build a Strong Family

If the wisdom of God is the principal tool for building a strong family, understanding how to access this divine wisdom becomes imperative. The Bible states:

> *For every house is builded by some man; but he that built all things is God.*
>
> HEBREWS *3:4 KJV*

Your family's strength is reflective of the wisdom it is built upon, akin to the house of David, which was stronger than the house of Saul due to David's adherence to Godly wisdom. This chapter will delve into accessing different dimensions of wisdom for a robust family foundation, drawing inspiration from biblical figures like Daniel, who accessed these dimensions of wisdom and became stronger than the ten leading citizens of Babylon as stated in:

> *One wise person is stronger than ten leading citizens of a town!*
>
> ECCLESIASTES *7:19 NLT*

What God did for Daniel, He is willing to do for others. Daniel's access to wisdom is not a relic of the past; it remains available through the Holy Spirit.

Wisdom is described as the principal spirit among the seven spirits of God. It empowers one to operate at the principal level of destiny.

> *And there shall come forth a rod out of the stem of Jesse, and a Branch shall grow out of his roots: And the spirit of the Lord shall rest upon him, the spirit of wisdom and understanding, the spirit of counsel and might, the spirit of knowledge and of the fear of the Lord;*
>
> ISAIAH 11:1-2

I believe, as you read this book, the same dimensions of wisdom that elevated Daniel and his colleagues will be granted to you. Just as Daniel enjoyed victories over satanic plotting through God's wisdom, may you also experience such victories in your family.

Wisdom in Action: The Example of Daniel

In the case of Daniel and his colleagues:

> *As for these four children, God gave them knowledge and skill in all learning and wisdom: and Daniel had understanding in all visions and dreams. Now at the end of the days...the king communed with them; and...he found them ten*

times better than all the magicians and astrologers that were in all his realm.

DANIEL 1:17-20

Daniel and his colleagues were given divine wisdom, elevating them above their peers. This wisdom is not limited to understanding and knowledge but extends to practical application in overcoming family challenges. The queen in Daniel's story, a non-believer, recognized the wisdom in Daniel, acknowledging its power in delivering the king's father from troubles.

Every family challenge is fundamentally a wisdom problem. There is no challenge that cannot be addressed through wisdom. It is my sincere belief that as you seek wisdom from God, as Daniel did, you too will receive it and experience the same level of dominion and victory in your family life.

Chapter 11

What Are The Different Dimensions Of Wisdom

Whatever God does for one, he is willing to do for others. If God gave Daniel those dimensions of wisdom, he can do the same for us. Daniel is gone, but those spirits are still here. There are different dimensions which are offshoots of the spirit of wisdom. The spirit of wisdom is an offshoot of the spirit of God.

God gave Daniel different dimensions in the operation of wisdom. That is why wisdom is the principal thing. It is the only dimension of the spirit that has many dimensional fruits and offshoots. Wisdom is the principal spirit among the seven spirits of God. (Isaiah 11:1-2) That is why you will never hear of different levels in the operation of knowledge, or understanding, or might like it is mentioned for wisdom. Only wisdom has many different operations because it is the principal spirit. When you have wisdom, it will empower you to operate at the principal level of destiny. That is why I believe that, as you read this book, God will give you the same dimensions of wisdom that made Daniel enjoy different dimensions of victory that only God could have made possible. God will give you those types of victories also in the name of Jesus Christ.

The Holy Spirit is here on the pages of this book to impart to you something that is lacking in your life called wisdom. As you read the Holy Spirit is here to put inside you something that will make you have a victorious life on the earth. He will impart strength and grace that will cause you to be better than your colleagues. That is what the Spirit made Daniel become.

> *7 But if the ministration of death, written and engraven in stones, was glorious, so that the children of Israel could not stedfastly behold the face of Moses for the glory of his countenance; which glory was to be done away: 8 How shall not the ministration of the spirit be rather glorious?*
>
> 2 Corinthians 3:7-8 KJV

If Daniel, an Old Testament believer without a complete Bible in his hands, could operate in this dimension of wisdom, how much more should we New Testament believers operate in this wisdom. Jesus said, I am in the Father and the Father is in me. (John 14:11). I can say I am in Jesus and Jesus is in me. I am in the Holy Ghost and the Holy Ghost is in me. This same Spirit will rest upon you and make you ten times better than your colleagues, ten times better in your realm, ten times better in your business, ten times better in your marriage, ten times better in your career. It will give you victory that only God can give, and make you go to your den of lions and come out to answer. It can make you go into the fiery furnace and come out to answer. Everyone who operated under this dimension operated with invincibility. That is why I believe that the same God that endowed Daniel will endow you and I today in Jesus's name.

In Daniel 1:5-6, Daniel was in training for three years. They were being trained in the wisdom of Babylon for operation in the palace. However, in Daniel 1:17-20, the Bible says:

17 As for these four children, God gave them knowledge and skill in all learning and wisdom: and Daniel had understanding in all visions and dreams. 18 Now at the end of the days that the king had said he should bring them in, then the prince of the eunuchs brought them in before Nebuchadnezzar. 19 And the king communed with them; and among them all was found none like Daniel, Hananiah, Mishael, and Azariah: therefore stood they before the king. 20 And in all matters of wisdom and understanding, that

> *the king enquired of them, he found them ten times better than all the magicians and astrologers that were in all his realm.*
>
> DANIEL *1:17-20 KJV*

Daniel and his colleagues were in school, and God gave them something that made them better than the other colleagues. That thing made them operate in the ten levels of wisdom. A university can only give you knowledge. Only God can give you wisdom. Wisdom is the grace to apply the things you know.

In Daniel 5:9, the king was troubled because he didn't remember nor understand the dream he had.

In Daniel 5:11-12, the queen saw Daniel and discerned and testified to operations of wisdom that were at work in Daniel.

The ten dimensions of wisdom can bring you out of trouble. To every trouble there is a wisdom solution to it. Don't let your countenance trouble you. Every challenge you have is a wisdom problem. There is no challenge and trouble you face that cannot be answered through wisdom.

The queen was not born again. She was a non-believer and idol worshipper, yet she could smell the different fragrances from Daniel. She told the king that it was wisdom that delivered the king's father when he was in trouble. So, the queen outlined these 10 dimensions of wisdom.

Following are 10 dimensions of wisdom that were at work in Daniel:

1. Light
2. Knowledge
3. Understanding
4. Wisdom
5. Spirit of Mastery
6. Supernatural Wisdom of God
7. Excellent Spirit
8. Interpretation of Dreams
9. Showing hard sentences
10. Dissolving Doubts

Dimension 1. Light

The first dimension that God gave Daniel was light.

> *11 There is a man in thy kingdom, in whom is the spirit of the holy gods; and in the days of thy father light and understanding and wisdom, like the wisdom of the gods, was found in him; whom the king Nebuchadnezzar thy father, the king, I say, thy father, made master of the magicians, astrologers, Chaldeans, and soothsayers;*
>
> DANIEL 5:11 KJV

If God gave the light dimension of wisdom to Daniel, he can give it to us as well. James 1:5 prayer brings wisdom.

> *If any of you lack wisdom, let him ask of God, that giveth to all men liberally, and upbraideth not; and it shall be given him.*
>
> JAMES 1:5 KJV

It will put you above your peers in your realm. When God sends light about something, you have a sudden burst of knowledge. All forms of darkness go out. Revelation comes.

> *That the God of our Lord Jesus Christ, the Father of glory, may give unto you the spirit of wisdom and revelation in the knowledge of him:*
>
> EPHESIANS 1:17 KJV

Paul, in this scripture, means that darkness will be exposed. The first dimension that God gave Daniel was light.

> *1 Arise, shine; for thy light is come, and the glory of the LORD is risen upon thee.*
>
> ISAIAH 60:1 KJV

Pray that your light is coming today. The Lord that gave light to Daniel concerning the dream of Nebuchadnezzar will also give you light.

> *19 Then was the secret revealed unto Daniel in a night vision. Then Daniel blessed the God of heaven. 20 Daniel answered and said, Blessed be the name of God for ever and ever: for wisdom and might are his: 21 And he changeth the times and the seasons: he removeth kings, and setteth up kings: he giveth wisdom unto the wise, and knowledge to them that know understanding: 22 He revealeth the deep and secret things: he knoweth what is in the darkness, and the light dwelleth with him.*
>
> DANIEL 2:19-22

The Lord will give you light that will expose darkness around you and expose the work of the devil. He will give you light in your business, light for your family, light for your marriage, light for your life and direction.

Say this prayer: *"Lord, I ask for this light today in the name Lord Jesus. Light that will give me mastery over decisions of life. God, you are light and wisdom. Let your light be activated in my life. Thank you Lord in Jesus's name."*

If you are not born again, remember that Jesus is light. He that follows me (Jesus) shall not walk in darkness.

> *Then spake Jesus again unto them, saying, I am the light of the world: he that followeth me shall not walk in darkness, but shall have the light of life.*
>
> JOHN 8:12

Prayer of salvation:

Lord Jesus, I come to you right now; forgive me of my sins, wash me with your blood and cleanse me today. I receive you as my Lord and Savior. Thank you for saving my soul in Jesus' mighty name. Amen

Dimension 2. Knowledge

Wisdom is applying what you know. So, knowledge is raw material for the application of wisdom.

You can have knowledge without wisdom, but you can't operate in wisdom without knowledge. So, when you don't know anything at all, there is nothing to apply. That is why Peter said when it comes to relationships, Husband, should dwell with wife accordingly...

> *Likewise, ye husbands, dwell with them according to knowledge, giving honour unto the wife, as unto the weaker vessel, and as being heirs together of the grace of life; that your prayers be not hindered.*
>
> 1 Peter 3:7

If you are ignorant, you can't enjoy family peace and you will have lack of peace. Successful relationships are rooted in knowledge and application of the word of God.

This was why Paul asked us to pray for revelation knowledge as expressed in Ephesians 1:17-18:

> *17 That the God of our Lord Jesus Christ, the Father of glory, may give unto you the spirit of wisdom and revelation in the knowledge of him: 18 The eyes of your understanding being enlightened; that ye may know what is the hope of his calling, and what the riches of the glory of his inheritance in the saints,*
>
> Ephesians 1:17-18 KJV

In the school of wisdom, knowledge is a very major force. Knowledge of the word of God is the rod that is needed to stir wisdom into manifestation. There are things you don't know that you begin to know by revelation knowledge.

> *The Lord's voice crieth unto the city, and the man of wisdom shall see thy name: hear ye the rod, and who hath appointed it.*
>
> MICAH 6:9 KJV

> Rod = word of God

There is connection between rod (word of God) and wisdom. Word of God is what stirs the wisdom deposit that is inside you to produce. It is the rod that is used to form a proper solution. Without the rod, you can't form a solution. A man of wisdom must bear the rod; he must feed on the rod of God's knowledge.

> *Feed thy people with thy rod, the flock of thine heritage, which dwell solitarily in the wood, in the midst of Carmel: let them feed in Bashan and Gilead, as in the days of old.*
>
> MICAH 7:14 KJV

I prophesy that grace to feed on the word, to hear the word and to understand it – receive that grace now in Jesus's name. Amen.

The word of God cannot be overemphasised because the Bible makes it very clear in Psalm 119:98

Thou through thy commandments hast made me wiser than mine enemies: for they are ever with me.

The word of God is the command of God and the force behind sound wisdom. The word of God that you have seen is the rod of knowledge that stirs up your mind into action. It ensures the proper mixing of the rich deposit of wisdom in you.

The hearing and the studying of God's word is feeding on it. It stirs the deposit of wisdom that you received by redemption. Pray that God will fill you with the knowledge of his will.

Lord, fill me with the knowledge of your will in all spiritual wisdom and understanding that I will be able to bear fruit – your will for this season, my life, my family, my business, for this season in which I am. Let me be a beneficiary of revelation knowledge that I need as I read and study your word. Thank you because you have answered Lord in Jesus's mighty name. Amen

Dimension 3. Understanding.

> *Understanding is the third dimension of wisdom.*

Understanding enhances the undertaking of any ventures including relationships. This spirit was at work in Daniel (Daniel 5:11). Understanding is a major part of wisdom, paired together.

With all thy getting, get understanding.

PROVERBS *4:7*

Daniel was one person God did not only give wisdom, but he also gave him understanding. In Daniel 10:10-14, Daniel sought the face of God in prayers to bring an end to 70 years of captivity. God didn't send an angel just to visit Daniel, but to give him understanding, the ability to comprehend and walk in understanding. The Lord then released the spirit of understanding.

Prayers unlock the spirit of understanding. Prayer time is time of understanding. In Ephesians 1:17-18, Paul tells us to pray that the eyes of our understanding be enlightened or floored with the light of the Holy Spirit.

The difference between men in life is in understanding. It takes understanding to walk out whatever prophetic word God has given you. Job 12:13 With him is wisdom and strength, he hath counsel and understanding. That is why the Bible tells us in Habakkuk 2:1-3 to write the vision and make it plain, understandable that he may run that reads it. Vision answers to runners; it enhances speed.

The reason many relationships and ventures fail is traceable to lack of understanding.

> *But he that received seed into the good ground is he that heareth the word, and understandeth it; which also beareth fruit, and bringeth forth, some an hundredfold, some sixty, some thirty*
>
> MATTHEW 13:23 KJV

The depth of understanding is what determines your level of fruitful. The more you understand, the more fruitfulness you will see in your life and relationships.

On the other hand, lack of understanding is the reason for barrenness in many relationships. The deeper your understanding, the more fruit you bear. The Bible also tells us, for instance, that he who commits adultery is due to lack understanding.

> *But whoso committeth adultery with a woman lacketh understanding:...*
>
> PROVERBS 6:32A KJV

Dimension 4. Wisdom

Wisdom is walking in the revealed ways of God. It was what was revealed to Daniel concerning Nebuchadnezzar's dream that bailed him out of destruction along with other magicians.

> *Then was the secret revealed unto Daniel in a night vision. Then Daniel blessed the God of heaven.*
>
> *DANIEL 2:19 KJV*

The wisdom that was revealed to Daniel was what revealed him to his world. Read how the man in the scripture below used wisdom to bring deliverance to a city.

> *There was a little city, and few men within it; and there came a great king against it, and besieged it, and built great bulwarks against it: now there was found in it a poor wise man, and he by his wisdom delivered the city; yet no man remembered that same poor man.*
>
> *ECCLESIASTES 9:14-15*

In the same vein, wisdom can help you to have profitable success faster than without it.

If the iron be blunt, and he do not whet the edge, then must he put to more strength: but wisdom is profitable to direct.

ECCLESIASTES 10:10

Give therefore thy servant an understanding heart to judge thy people, that I may discern between good and bad: for who is able to judge this thy so great a people? And the speech pleased the Lord, that Solomon had asked this thing. And God said unto him, Because thou hast asked this thing, and hast not asked for thyself long life; neither hast asked riches for thyself, nor hast asked the life of thine enemies; but hast asked for thyself understanding to discern judgment; behold, I have done according to thy words: lo, I have given thee a wise and an understanding heart; so that there was none like thee before thee, neither after thee shall any arise like unto thee.

1 KINGS 3:9-12

Prayer for wisdom will always please God as we saw in Solomon's prayer, and wisdom will bring other blessings you did not ask for. That is why the Bible sates that wisdom is the principal thing (Proverbs 4:7).

Dimensions 5. Spirit of Mastery

> *Whom your father made the master of magicians, astrologers*
>
> DANIEL 5:11 KJV

Daniel had mastery over all the magicians. This dimension of wisdom will give you mastery over challenges, mastery over wickedness, mastery over the magicians (to be on top of the current magic of the day; to be a master of the current ideas of the times). Anywhere the wisdom of God is, it gives you mastery over whatever situations of life you are facing.

Pray: *Lord, give me mastery over the current magic of my day. Give me mastery over the situations and challenges I am facing right now. Master over wickedness, master over principalities and powers, mastery to put all those devils where they belong. I receive mastery to be in charge, puts me higher than diabolical forces.*

> *To the intent that now unto the principalities and powers in heavenly places might be known by the church the manifold wisdom of God.*
>
> EPHESIANS 3:10 KJV

Dimension 6. Supernatural Wisdom of God

> *There is a man in thy kingdom, in whom is the spirit of the holy gods; and in the days of thy father light and understanding and wisdom, like the wisdom of the gods, was found in him; whom the king Nebuchadnezzar thy father, the king, I say, thy father, made master of the magicians, astrologers, Chaldeans, and soothsayers;*
>
> **DANIEL 5:11**

This is super human wisdom, this is wisdom from above, superior to intellectual wisdom, diabolical wisdom and natural wisdom, operating in God's revealed ways to make waves on the earth.

> *8 For my thoughts are not your thoughts, neither are your ways my ways, saith the Lord. 9 For as the heavens are higher than the earth, so are my ways higher than your ways, and my thoughts than your thoughts.*
>
> **ISAIAH 55:8-9**

This is this kind of wisdom that says give if you want to see increase and worldly wisdom says keep to see increase, it does not make sense because this kind of instruction does not come from sense realm.

Pray for this type of wisdom. This kind of wisdom will affect the way you think. Daniel engaged this wisdom to deliver the king from a national crisis, and it will deliver you from your own crisis too, if you ask God for it. It will cause your life to be better and open you up to God's way of thinking.

Prayer points:

1. *Lord, give me the supernatural wisdom--to see things the way you see things. You gave it to Daniel, give it to me. Give me light, wisdom, and understanding in the name of Jesus Christ.*

2. *Lord give me the wisdom to be able to overturn mountains of crises from the root. Thank you Lord Jesus.*

Understanding is the force that determines fruitfulness.

Dimension 7. Spirit of Excellence

> *Forasmuch as an excellent spirit, and knowledge, and understanding, interpreting of dreams, and shewing of hard sentences, and dissolving of doubts, were found in the same Daniel, whom*

*the king named Belteshazzar: now let Daniel be
called, and he will shew the interpretation.*

***Daniel* 5:12 KJV**

Excellent Spirit is one of the effects of the operation of wisdom in a human spirit; it will make you excel.

Excellent Spirit is a sweet spirit that is free of bitterness. When you are bitter it affects the way you respond to things. It makes you salty. The only thing that grows on salty ground is coconut. If you have a salty spirit or wounded spirit, you don't have an excellent spirit. You will see things through your hurt. It affects your perception which determines your reception. When you receive a word, it corrupts that word because your heart is not free.

An excellent spirit is free from anger, bitterness, and revenge. You need the dimension of excellent spirit to have peaceful relationships in your life. Ask God to give you an excellent spirit (James 1:5).

*If any of you lack wisdom, let him ask of God,
that giveth to all men liberally, and upbraideth
not; and it shall be given him.*

***James* 1:5 KJV**

Your background can affect your relationships. Someone with a wounded spirit will leak on other people and wound others, even those who had nothing to do with the problem. An excellent spirit will empower you to develop a good attitude. You can be burnt and not bitter. Some people, by virtue of the problems they face in their life (they have been abandoned, things have not worked for them), they grow bitter. When you have a bitter spirit, you cannot have an excellent spirit. You can't be bitter and be bigger or better in life. You must be free from anger, bitterness, vengefulness, and quarrelsome spirit. There are people that fight every day of their life. It's almost like working for a security company, CIA, they are suspicious of everybody. Our background determines how we receive words (reception). That is why some people need to pray for an excellent spirit.

An excellent spirit is also a spirit that makes you excel. Pray for that spirit because without it, you will not excel in your journey of life. The wisdom of God will not stay where there is bitterness, anger, nor vengefulness. Read from the book of James (James 3:13-15). You will see that the kind of wineskin that carries wisdom must have an excellent spirit, meaning a good attitude. For example, a bottle of water must be pure in order to carry pure water. Hence, your spirit must also be clean. Wisdom is like water; the bottle is like your spirit. If the bottle (your spirit) is dirty, you cannot put water (wisdom) inside it. So, when you don't have an excellent spirit, the wisdom of God cannot stay inside of you. It takes an excellent spirit to excel in life.

> *Then this Daniel was preferred above the presidents and princes, because an excellent spirit was in him; and the king thought to set him over the whole realm.*
>
> DANIEL 6:3 KJV

An excellent spirit makes you excel anywhere you are. It puts you above others. It means you will be distinguished. Remember, Daniel was in captivity, but he was not a captive. He was an immigrant who lived like a prince. (Daniel 5:11) That same spirit was found in Joseph.

> *And Pharaoh said unto his servants, Can we find such a one as this is, a man in whom the Spirit of God is?*
>
> GENESIS 41:38

They both had the spirit of excellence in them. Although Joseph was sold into slavery, he didn't live like a slave, nor act like a slave and didn't have a slave mentality. Joseph was in prison, but he was not a prisoner. Notice everything about life is attitude. You can go through hard times, but don't allow the hard times to make you a hard man. You can go through bad things, don't let bad things make you a bad man. You can be burnt and not bitter. Joseph always walked in the excellent spirit—always smiling, always excited. Some people walk around with their problems on their face. Don't be always moody and sad. You need an excellent spirit which gives you the ability to have a good attitude even when things are not going well with you.

Pray for an excellent spirit – helps you to keep a good attitude even though things are not going well. That attitude will keep the spirit of wisdom around you. Clean your spirit so you can be free from retaliation. Joseph was thrown in prison and was lied on, but he did not take revenge against his brothers. You can't keep unforgiveness or bitterness in your heart and keep God there. Some people say I forgive but I can't forget. You can't keep an unforgiving spirit and keep the spirit of wisdom.

> *The fear of God will also keep an excellent spirit.*

> *And Joseph said unto them the third day, This do, and live; for I fear God:*
>
> GENESIS *42:18 KJV*

An excellent spirit is an offshoot of the fear of God. You must have a clean heart.

Daniel and Joseph excelled wherever they were because of the spirit of excellent inside of them. When you have an excellent spirit, no matter the prison or lion's den you are put in, you will come out of it. Excellent spirit will not allow you to die in your prison nor your sickness. You can be sick and not have a sickly attitude.

Prayer Points:

1. *Lord, give me an excellent spirit – free from suspicion, pride, lust, wicked spirit. Give me a humble spirit.*

2. *Ask God to heal your wounded spirit so you can have an excellent spirit which will give you an excellent attitude.*

Some people don't trust anybody. If you say good morning, they will wonder why you said good morning to them. It is as if they work for a security company because they are seeing through wounded eyes. They have been wounded and not healed so they take out their wounds on everyone.

> *Attitude is your approach to life.*
> *Your viewpoint on life.*

An excellent spirit is a new wineskin spirit. The new wineskin is what you need to carry the Holy Spirit.

> *30 And grieve not the Holy Spirit of God, whereby ye are sealed unto the day of redemption. 31 Let all bitterness, and wrath, and anger, and clamor, and evil speaking, be put away from you, with all malice:*
>
> Ephesians *4:30-31 KJV*

An excellent spirit is free from bitterness, wrath, anger, clamour, evil speaking and malice.

> *30 And grieve not the holy Spirit of God, whereby ye are sealed unto the day of redemption. 31 Let all bitterness, and wrath, and anger, and clamour, and evil speaking, be put away from you, with all malice: 32 And be ye kind one to another, tenderhearted, forgiving one another, even as God for Christ's sake hath forgiven you.*
>
> Ephesians *4:30-32 KJV*

You are correctable.

When you are too tough or coconut head because of bitterness and anger or sinful life, you have a hardened heart. You are a hard person to deal with relationship wise. So, ask God to purge you of anti-excellent spirit.

> *21 If a man therefore purge himself from these, he shall be a vessel unto honour, sanctified, and meet for the master's use, and prepared unto every good work. 22 Flee also youthful lusts: but follow righteousness, faith, charity, peace, with them that call on the Lord out of a pure heart.*
>
> *2 Tim 2:21-22 KJV*

So, follow after love, peace and righteousness

> *Excellent spirit is a lifestyle.*

> *4 Then the presidents and princes sought to find occasion against Daniel concerning the kingdom; but they could find none occasion nor fault; forasmuch as he was faithful, neither was there any error or fault found in him.*
>
> *Daniel 6:4 KJV*

Faithful and no errors found in him, reliable, not deceptive, not backstabbers, you trust with an assignment and sleep, integrity, their word is their bond, dependable

> *Then said these men, We shall not find any occasion against this Daniel, except we find it against him concerning the law of his God.*
> *DANIEL 6:5 KJV*

Those with an excellent spirit are lovers of God. Daniel was a man of prayer that sought God. Even though he was in a high political position, he did not allow his status to turn him into a statue.

Daniel lived like a prince even though he was a captive from Judah in the land, meaning an immigrant, yet without a captive-mentality.

He served God and He used his position to serve God and advance God's kingdom. Use everything God has put in your possession to serve Him--talent, treasure, and time. You don't have to be a pastor to be a servant of God. Not bossy, not peacockish, not proud, nor arrogant; they are humble that is why grace comes for them. Anything they do for the kingdom they consider a privilege.

Prayer Point: *Lord, give me the excellent spirit that you gave to Daniel, Joseph, Jesus, and Paul. Lord,* *give it to me. A spirit free of bitterness, malice; let my heart not be an habitat where people are imprisoned.*

> *11 There is a man in thy kingdom, in whom is the spirit of the holy gods; and in the days of thy father light and understanding and wisdom, like the wisdom of the gods, was found in him; whom the king Nebuchadnezzar thy father, the king, I say, thy father, made master of the magicians, astrologers, Chaldeans, and soothsayers; 12 Forasmuch as an excellent spirit, and knowledge, and understanding, interpreting of dreams, and shewing of hard sentences, and dissolving of doubts, were found in the same Daniel, whom the king named Belteshazzar: now let Daniel be called, and he will shew the interpretation.*
>
> DANIEL 5:11-12 KJV

Wisdom is the Holy Spirit within you. The power of God is the Holy Spirit upon you.

> *But the anointing which ye have received of him abideth in you, and ye need not that any man teach you: but as the same anointing teacheth you of all things, and is truth, and is no lie, and even as it hath taught you, ye shall abide in him.*
>
> 1 JOHN 2:27 KJV

Dimension 8. Interpretation of Dreams

Many people have dreams but don't understand them. Interpretation helps you to remember.

God speaks to us in dreams; he gives us intelligence. Sometimes dreams come in the form of a trance. Dreams are God's guidance for your life. If Joseph, the husband of Mary, did not understand dreams, he would not have been the earthly father of Jesus. Joseph planned to quietly walk away from Mary before the wedding. An angel of the Lord appeared to Joseph in a dream and said:

> *Joseph, son of David, do not be afraid to take Mary as your wife, for the child conceived in her is from the Holy Spirit."*
>
> MATTHEW 1:21 KJV

Joseph had 4 dreams, one of them saved Jesus from death. Herod wanted to kill that child; it was God who said carry the child and run away because they wanted to destroy his child.

Your dream life must be restored because God wants that medium to speak to you. The ability to have and understand dreams is wisdom. It takes wisdom to interpret dreams. It is like spiritual theatre, where you are watching the event going on in your life in the realm of the spirit. This is what gave Joseph deliverance from crisis. Pharoah would have killed all the magicians and all the wise men if his dream had not been interpreted. This wisdom spirit interpreted the dream of Pharoah.

Ask God for the grace to be able to dream and interpret your dreams. I pray for grace to be able to dream and interpret your dream. Receive it in Jesus's name. It is part of the operation of the wisdom of God.

> *And it shall come to pass afterward, that I will pour out my spirit upon all flesh; and your sons and your daughters shall prophesy, your old men shall dream dreams, your young men shall see visions:*
>
> *JOEL 2:28 KJV*

In Daniel 2, interpretation of dreams was used to deliver Daniel from Nebuchadnezzer's decree to kill all wise men.

> *17 Then Daniel went to his house, and made the thing known to Hananiah, Mishael, and Azariah, his companions: 18 That they would desire mercies of the God of heaven concerning this secret; that Daniel and his fellows should not perish with the rest of the wise men of Babylon. 19 Then was the secret revealed unto Daniel in*

a night vision. Then Daniel blessed the God of heaven.

DANIEL 2:17-19 KJV

God uses dreams to talk to you, giving you intelligence. You can't even talk about Joseph and his brothers without talking about dreams. The ability to interpret dreams took Joseph from prison to the palace. "Can we find a man like this, in whom is the Spirit of God?" Genesis 41:38. This chamber of wisdom is what helps you to interpret dreams. I pray that you receive that grace in Jesus's name.

Dimension 9. Showing of Hard Sentences

For as much as an excellent spirit, and knowledge, and understanding, interpreting of dreams, and shewing of hard sentences, and dissolving of doubts, were found in the same Daniel, whom the king named Belteshazzar: now let Daniel be called, and he will shew the interpretation.

DANIEL 5:12 KJV

There are times when God will give you hard sentences. Your ability to be able to deal with them enables you to become who you are meant to be in life.

There are different kinds of hard sentences.

1. Hard Rebuke.

Hard sentences can come from rebuke. When a person rebukes you for what you are doing wrong, it is your ability to embrace that rebuke and improve that can be a turning point in your life. Some people don't like to be corrected. When you react to correction, it is evidence of how far God can take you. Some people react even though they know what that person is saying is true. You may have a character issue that you are struggling with, and you know it is wrong, yet you are fighting to defend it. For example, you are given to anger, but you walk away when someone tries to correct you.

When Jesus taught on communion in John 6:60, people turned away from him because they said it was too hard for them. How can you say we are eating your flesh and drinking your blood? Are you a witch? Many turned away, but the disciples stayed, and it turned their lives around. So, a hard sentence can come from rebuke. Some people will dismiss you even though it is something that will turn their lives around.

2. Dismissal.

This is, for example, when an individual is fired from a job because of wrong doings. If that person learns from the consequences of that mistake, it becomes a turning point in their life.

Some people may have to be dismissed or let go before a turning point can happen in their lives. This type of situation can bring you to your wits end, and God will use the hard situation to bring you to the place of brokenness before him for God's help to show up in your life.

3. Wrong lane or wrong doing.

Another hard sentences is when you are told you are in the wrong lane or doing the wrong thing. wrong relationship. For example, someone may say that you are in a wrong relationship. Letting go of someone you love is hard. That relationship may land you in trouble. It may be that your blood types don't match. If you have children with that person, you will have issues with your children. Your ability to embrace that correction will help you to avoid crises later and live a better life in the future.

4. Judgment of people.

Like people in court are sentenced to prison.

5. Curses

This is what happened to Adam. God told Adam not to eat of the tree of knowledge of good and evil. Because of his disobedience, Adam was sentenced to eat through painful toil. That is a hard sentence.

6. Hard instructions

God gives you an assignment. God told me to go to America, and I obeyed. Because of that obedience, it was a turning point in my life. Or God may tell you to give a sacrifice. When you obey, it will turn your life around. Hard instructions are hard realities.

7. Hard prophecy

You expect a positive prophecy, but some prophecies can be negative. If you embrace that prophecy, your life will have a turnaround.

> *16 So then because thou art lukewarm, and neither cold nor hot, I will spue thee out of my mouth. 17 Because thou sayest, I am rich, and increased with goods, and have need of nothing; and knowest not that thou art wretched, and miserable, and poor, and blind, and naked:*
>
> *REVELATION 3:16-17 KJV*

Dimension 10. Dissolving of Doubt

God dissolves doubt so you can have faith. Faith is in what you believe. This will affect your life. When what you believe is part of your wisdom. Daniel spoke to the king by faith of what was written on the wall, and it dissolved their doubts.

> *For as much as an excellent spirit, and knowledge, and understanding, interpreting of dreams, and shewing of hard sentences, and dissolving of doubts, were found in the same Daniel, whom the king named Belteshazzar: now let Daniel be called, and he will shew the interpretation.*
>
> *Daniel 5:12 KJV*

Pray: *Lord, I ask for the spirit of wisdom so my doubts can be dissolved.*

As we walk in these things, I see the ten dimensions operating in your life in Jesus's name.

Pray: *Lord, I receive light from heaven, knowledge, Understanding, mastery over principalities and powers, supernatural wisdom, spirit of excellence, grace to interpret my dreams, grace to cope with hard sentences, and grace to dissolve doubt. I receive them in Jesus's name. Amen.*

Chapter 12

Twenty-One Facts About Wisdom for Building a Strong Family

Fact one

Wisdom is the first thing you must possess at the beginning of building a strong family

The LORD possessed me in the beginning of his way, Before his works of old.

PROVERBS 8:22

I love them that love me; and those that seek me early shall find me.

PROVERBS 8:1

And the child grew, and waxed strong in spirit, filled with wisdom: and the grace of God was upon him.

LUKE 2:40

Fact two

The first dimension of wisdom is light

There is a man in thy kingdom, in whom is the spirit of the holy gods; and in the days of thy father light and understanding and wisdom, like the wisdom of the gods, was found in him; whom the king Nebuchadnezzar thy father, the king, I say, thy father, made master of the magicians, astrologers, Chaldeans, and soothsayers;

Daniel 5:11

In the beginning God created the heaven and the earth. And the earth was without form, and void; and darkness was upon the face of the deep. And the Spirit of God moved upon the face of the waters.

3 And God said, Let there be light: and there was light.

Genesis 1:1-3

That the God of our Lord Jesus Christ, the Father of glory, may give unto you the spirit of wisdom and revelation in the knowledge of him: The eyes of your understanding being enlightened; that ye may know what is the hope of his calling, and what the riches of the glory of his inheritance in the saints.

Ephesians 1:17-18

Fact three

The longevity and health of every marriage and family is determined by wisdom.

Length of days is in her right hand; and in her left hand riches and honour.

PROVERBS 3:16

Because he hath set his love upon me, therefore will I deliver him: I will set him on high, because he hath known my name.

PSALMS 91:14

Fact four

The mantle of wisdom makes you ten times stronger than those without it.

Wisdom strengtheneth the wise more than ten mighty men which are in the city.

ECCLESIASTES *7:19*

17 As for these four children, God gave them knowledge and skill in all learning and wisdom: and Daniel had understanding in all visions and dreams. 18 Now at the end of the days that the king had said he should bring them in, then the prince of the eunuchs brought them in before Nebuchadnezzar. 19 And the king communed with them; and among them all was found none like Daniel, Hananiah, Mishael, and Azariah: therefore stood they before the king. 20 And in all matters of wisdom and understanding, that the king enquired of them, he found them ten times better than all the magicians and astrologers that were in all his realm.

DANIEL *1:17-20*

3 Through wisdom is an house builded; and by understanding it is established: 4 And by knowledge shall the chambers be filled with all precious and pleasant riches. 5 A wise man is strong; yea, a man of knowledge increaseth strength.

PROVERBS *24:3-5*

Fact five

Wisdom is the holy spirit at work within you.

38 And Pharaoh said unto his servants, Can we find such a one as this is, a man in whom the Spirit of God is? 39 And Pharaoh said unto Joseph, Forasmuch as God hath shewed thee all this, there is none so discreet and wise as thou art: 40 Thou shalt be over my house, and according unto thy word shall all my people be ruled: only in the throne will I be greater than thou.

Genesis 41:38-40

11 There is a man in thy kingdom, in whom is the spirit of the holy gods; and in the days of thy father light and understanding and wisdom, like the wisdom of the gods, was found in him; whom the king Nebuchadnezzar thy father, the king, I say, thy father, made master of the magicians, astrologers, Chaldeans, and soothsayers;

Daniel 5:11

But ye have an unction from the Holy One, and ye know all things.

1 John 2:20

But the anointing which ye have received of him abideth in you, and ye need not that any man teach you: but as the same anointing teacheth you of all things, and is truth, and is no lie, and even as it hath taught you, ye shall abide in him.

1 John 2:27

The Spirit of the Lord is upon me, because he hath anointed me to preach the gospel to the poor; he hath sent me to heal the brokenhearted, to preach deliverance to the captives, and recovering of sight to the blind, to set at liberty them that are bruised

Luke 4:18

Fact six

The holy spirit is the spirit of wisdom that unleashes your gifts, talents and skills.

1 And the Lord spake unto Moses, saying, 2 See, I have called by name Bezaleel the son of Uri, the son of Hur, of the tribe of Judah: 3 And I have filled him with the spirit of God, in wisdom, and in understanding, and in knowledge, and in all manner of workmanship, 4 To devise cunning works, to work in gold, and in silver, and in brass,

Exodus 31:1-4

Then wrought Bezaleel and Aholiab, and every wise hearted man, in whom the Lord put wisdom and understanding to know how to work all manner of work for the service of the sanctuary, according to all that the Lord had commanded.

Exodus 36:1

Children in whom was no blemish, but well favoured, and skilful in all wisdom, and cunning in knowledge, and understanding science, and such as had ability in them to stand in the king's palace, and whom they might teach the learning and the tongue of the Chaldeans.

Daniel 1:4

Fact seven

A wise person will always be a person of peace.

But the wisdom that is from above is first pure, then peaceable, gentle, and easy to be intreated, full of mercy and good fruits, without partiality, and without hypocrisy.

JAMES 3:17

19 Brethren, if any of you do err from the truth, and one convert him; 20 Let him know, that he which converteth the sinner from the error of his way shall save a soul from death, and shall hide a multitude of sins.

JAMES 5:19-20

1 Brethren, if a man be overtaken in a fault, ye which are spiritual, restore such an one in the spirit of meekness; considering thyself, lest thou also be tempted. 2 Bear ye one another's burdens, and so fulfil the law of Christ.

GALATIANS 6:1-2

Fact eight

The evidence of wisdom in a relationship is the presence of peace, pleasantness and joy.

But the wisdom that is from above is first pure, then peaceable, gentle, and easy to be intreated, full of mercy and good fruits, without partiality, and without hypocrisy.

JAMES 3:17

Happy is the man that findeth wisdom, and the man that getteth understanding.

PROVERB 3:13

For wisdom is a defence, and money is a defence: but the excellency of knowledge is, that wisdom giveth life to them that have it.

ECCLESIASTES 7:12

Great peace have they which love thy law: and nothing shall offend them.

PSALMS 119:165

Fact nine

Wisdom gives you victory over your enemies and makes your adversaries helpless.

For I will give you a mouth and wisdom, which all your adversaries shall not be able to gainsay nor resist.

LUKE 21:15

For wisdom is a defence, and money is a defence: but the excellency of knowledge is, that wisdom giveth life to them that have it.

ECCLESIASTES 7:12

20 And when he came to the den, he cried with a lamentable voice unto Daniel: and the king spake and said to Daniel, O Daniel, servant of the living God, is thy God, whom thou servest continually, able to deliver thee from the lions? 21 Then said Daniel unto the king, O king, live for ever. 22 My God hath sent his angel, and hath shut the lions' mouths, that they have not hurt me: forasmuch as before him innocency was found in me; and also before thee, O king, have I done no hurt. 23 Then was the king exceedingly glad for him, and commanded that they should take Daniel up out of the den. So Daniel was taken up out of the den, and no manner of hurt was found upon him, because he believed in his God. 24 And the king commanded, and they brought those men which had accused Daniel, and they cast them into the den of lions, them, their children, and their wives; and the lions had the mastery of them, and brake all their bones in pieces or ever they came at the bottom of the den.

DANIEL 6:20-24

15 Now there was found in it a poor wise man, and he by his wisdom delivered the city; yet no man remembered that same poor man. 16 Then said I, Wisdom is better than strength: nevertheless the poor man's wisdom is despised, and his words are not heard. 17 The words of wise men are heard in quiet more than the cry of him that ruleth among fools. 18 Wisdom is better than weapons of war: but one sinner destroyeth much good.

ECCLESIASTES 9:15-18

Fact ten

A wise person is humble and open to correction.

When pride cometh, then cometh shame: but with the lowly is wisdom.

PROVERBS 11:2

11 My son, despise not the chastening of the Lord; neither be weary of his correction: 12 For whom the Lord loveth he correcteth; even as a father the son in whom he delighteth.

PROVERBS 3:11-12

31 The ear that heareth the reproof of life abideth among the wise. 32 He that refuseth instruction despiseth his own soul: but he that heareth reproof getteth understanding.

PROVERBS 15:31-32

8 Reprove not a scorner, lest he hate thee: rebuke a wise man, and he will love thee. Give instruction to a wise man, and he will be yet wiser: teach a just man, and he will increase in learning.

PROVERBS 9:8-9

Fact eleven

Wisdom is given to whoever asks god for it.

5 If any of you lack wisdom, let him ask of God, that giveth to all men liberally, and upbraideth not; and it shall be given him. 6 But let him ask in faith, nothing wavering. For he that wavereth is like a wave of the sea driven with the wind and tossed.

JAMES 1:5-6

17 Then Daniel went to his house, and made the thing known to Hananiah, Mishael, and Azariah, his companions: 18 That they would desire mercies of the God of heaven concerning this secret; that Daniel and his fellows should not perish with the rest of the wise men of Babylon. 19 Then was the secret revealed unto Daniel in a night vision. Then Daniel blessed the God of heaven.

DANIEL 2:17-19

7 Ask, and it shall be given you; seek, and ye shall find; knock, and it shall be opened unto you: 8

For every one that asketh receiveth; and he that seeketh findeth; and to him that knocketh it shall be opened. 9 Or what man is there of you, whom if his son ask bread, will he give him a stone? 10 Or if he ask a fish, will he give him a serpent? 11 If ye then, being evil, know how to give good gifts unto your children, how much more shall your Father which is in heaven give good things to them that ask him?

MATTHEW 7:7-11

Fact twelve

Prayer for wisdom is one of the greatest prayer that pleases god.

9 Give therefore thy servant an understanding heart to judge thy people, that I may discern between good and bad: for who is able to judge this thy so great a people? 10 And the speech pleased the Lord, that Solomon had asked this thing.

1 Kings 3:9-10

Fact thirteen

Prayer for wisdom is the kind of prayer that answers other prayers.

11 And God said unto him, Because thou hast asked this thing, and hast not asked for thyself long life; neither hast asked riches for thyself, nor hast asked the life of thine enemies; but hast asked for thyself understanding to discern judgment; 12 Behold, I have done according to thy words: lo, I have given thee a wise and an understanding heart; so that there was none like thee before thee, neither after thee shall any arise like unto thee. 13 And I have also given thee that which thou hast not asked, both riches, and honour: so that there shall not be any among the kings like unto thee all thy days.

1 Kings 3:11-13

13 Happy is the man that findeth wisdom, and the man that getteth understanding. 14 For the merchandise of it is better than the merchandise of silver, and the gain thereof than fine gold. 15 She is more precious than rubies: and all the things thou canst desire are not to be compared unto her. 16 Length of days is in her right hand; and in her left hand riches and honour. 17 Her ways are ways of pleasantness, and all her paths are peace.

Proverbs 3:13-17

Fact fourteen

A wise person's words carries healing.

Pleasant words are as an honeycomb, sweet to the soul, and health to the bones.

PROVERBS 16:24

5 Trust in the Lord with all thine heart; and lean not unto thine own understanding. 6 In all thy ways acknowledge him, and he shall direct thy paths. 7 Be not wise in thine own eyes: fear the Lord, and depart from evil. 8 It shall be health to thy navel, and marrow to thy bones.

PROVERBS 3:5-8

There is that speaketh like the piercings of a sword: but the tongue of the wise is health.

PROVERBS 12:18

20 A man's belly shall be satisfied with the fruit of his mouth; and with the increase of his lips shall he be filled. 21 Death and life are in the power of the tongue: and they that love it shall eat the fruit thereof.

PROVERBS 18:20-21

Fact fifteen

Wise association can increase wisdom in your life.

He that walketh with wise men shall be wise: but a companion of fools shall be destroyed.

Proverbs 13:20

17 Then Daniel went to his house, and made the thing known to Hananiah, Mishael, and Azariah, his companions: 18 That they would desire mercies of the God of heaven concerning this secret; that Daniel and his fellows should not perish with the rest of the wise men of Babylon.

Daniel 2:17-18

17 As for these four children, God gave them knowledge and skill in all learning and wisdom: and Daniel had understanding in all visions and dreams. 18 Now at the end of the days that the king had said he should bring them in, then the prince of the eunuchs brought them in before Nebuchadnezzar. 19 And the king communed with them; and among them all was found none like Daniel, Hananiah, Mishael, and Azariah: therefore stood they before the king. 20 And in all matters of wisdom and understanding, that the king enquired of them, he found them ten times better than all the magicians and astrologers that were in all his realm.

Daniel 1:17-20

Fact sixteen

Wisdom is a tool you use to build a strong family.

3 Through wisdom is an house builded; and by understanding it is established: 4 And by knowledge shall the chambers be filled with all precious and pleasant riches. 5 A wise man is strong; yea, a man of knowledge increaseth strength.

                                                  Proverbs 24:3-5

1 Wisdom hath builded her house, she hath hewn out her seven pillars: 2 She hath killed her beasts; she hath mingled her wine; she hath also furnished her table.

                                                    Proverbs 9:1-2

Fact seventeen

Wisdom stabilizes family relationships

And wisdom and knowledge shall be the stability of thy times, and strength of salvation: the fear of the Lord is his treasure.

Isaiah 33:6

24 Therefore whosoever heareth these sayings of mine, and doeth them, I will liken him unto a wise man, which built his house upon a rock: 25 And the rain descended, and the floods came, and the winds blew, and beat upon that house; and it fell not: for it was founded upon a rock. 26 And every one that heareth these sayings of mine, and doeth them not, shall be likened unto a foolish man, which built his house upon the sand:

Matthew 7:24-26

Fact eighteen

The word of God is the source of wisdom

Therefore also said the wisdom of God, I will send them prophets and apostles, and some of them they shall slay and persecute:

LUKE 11:49

5 Behold, I have taught you statutes and judgments, even as the Lord my God commanded me, that ye should do so in the land whither ye go to possess it. 6 Keep therefore and do them; for this is your wisdom and your understanding in the sight of the nations, which shall hear all these statutes, and say, Surely this great nation is a wise and understanding people.

DEUTERONOMY 4: 5-6

Therefore whosoever heareth these sayings of mine, and doeth them, I will liken him unto a wise man, which built his house upon a rock:

MATTHEW 7:24

Thou through thy commandments hast made me wiser than my enemies: for they are ever with me.

PSALM 119:98

Fact nineteen

How much wisdom you possess is revealed in your conversation.

Who is a wise man and endued with knowledge among you? let him shew out of a good conversation his works with meekness of wisdom.

James 3:13

Death and life are in the power of the tongue: and they that love it shall eat the fruit thereof.

Proverbs 18:21

And all the earth sought to Solomon, to hear his wisdom, which God had put in his heart.

1 Kings 10:24

Fact twenty

The wisdom of god is hidden and can only be revealed by the holy spirit.

6 Howbeit we speak wisdom among them that are perfect: yet not the wisdom of this world, nor of the princes of this world, that come to nought: 7 But we speak the wisdom of God in a mystery, even the hidden wisdom, which God ordained before the world unto our glory: 8 Which none of the princes of this world knew: for had they known it, they would not have crucified the Lord of glory. 9 But as it is written, Eye hath not seen, nor ear heard, neither have entered into the heart of man, the things which God hath prepared for them that love him. 10 But God hath revealed them unto us by his Spirit: for the Spirit searcheth all things, yea, the deep things of God. 11 For what man knoweth the things of a man, save the spirit of man which is in him? even so the things of God knoweth no man, but the Spirit of God.

1 Corinthians 2:6-11

1 And there shall come forth a rod out of the stem of Jesse, and a Branch shall grow out of his roots: 2 And the spirit of the Lord shall rest upon him, the spirit of wisdom and understanding, the spirit of counsel and might, the spirit of knowledge and of the fear of the Lord; 3 And shall make him of quick understanding in the fear of the Lord: and he shall not judge after the sight of his eyes, neither reprove after the hearing of his ears:

Isaiah 11:1-3

Fact twenty-one

Wisdom is accessible by those who fear god.

And unto man he said, Behold, the fear of the Lord, that is wisdom; and to depart from evil is understanding.

                                                             JOB **28:28**

The fear of the Lord is the beginning of wisdom: and the knowledge of the holy is understanding.

                                                        PROVERBS **9:10**

5 Then shalt thou understand the fear of the Lord, and find the knowledge of God. 6 For the Lord giveth wisdom: out of his mouth cometh knowledge and understanding.

                                                         PROVERBS **2:5-6**

You are warmly invited to join us at Destiny Church for All Nations in London!

If our testimony and work with the homeless community in London have inspired you, we would be delighted to have you witness our outreach efforts first-hand.

Sunday Services:
- **1st Service (Jesus Breakfast):** 9:00 AM
- **Destiny Moulding Service (2nd Service):** 10:30 AM

Venue:
Destiny Church for All Nations London, Deptford Adventure Playground Centre, New King Road, Deptford, London, SE8 3JB, United Kingdom.

Virtual Programs:
- **Wednesday:** Virtual Recovery of Destiny Program with our Senior Pastor.
- **Thursday:** Prayers for the Success of Businesses & Careers in the Marketplace.

Broadcast Time: 8:00 PM (UK Time) on:
- Adebo & Hyelazira Tomomewo Global Ministries Facebook Live.
- Destiny Mandate TV on YouTube.

Midweek Friday Service:
Hour of Destiny Prayer and Communion Service
Zoom ID: 5303778530 at 7:00 PM UK / 2:00 PM US EST. Continued on Adebo & Hyelazira Global Ministries Facebook page & Destiny Mandate TV on YouTube at 8:00 PM UK / 3:00 PM US EST.

For more details and to find our venue, please visit our website: **http://www.destinychurchnations.org**

Contact Us: +44 795 095 0815

We look forward to welcoming you to our community!

You are cordially invited to join us at Destiny Church for All Nations in Washington D.C.!

If you are in the USA and wish to worship with us, we warmly welcome you to our services.

Sunday Services:
1st Service: 9:30 AM
2nd Service: 10:30 AM

Venue:
5209 Georgia Avenue NW,
Washington, D.C. 20111

Virtual Programs:
Wednesday: Virtual Recovery of Destiny Program with our Senior Pastor.
Thursday: Prayers for the Success of Businesses & Careers in the Marketplace.

Broadcast Time: 8:00 PM (US EST) on:
- Adebo & Hyelazira Tomomewo Global Ministries Facebook Live.
- Destiny Mandate TV on YouTube.

Midweek Friday Service: Hour of Destiny Prayer and Communion Service
Zoom ID: 5303778530 at 7:00 PM UK / 2:00 PM US EST.
Continued on Adebo & Hyelazira Global Ministries Facebook page & Destiny Mandate TV on YouTube at 8:00 PM UK / 3:00 PM US EST.

Contact for More Information:
Minister Wanda Lofton, Minister-in-Charge
Phone: +1-240-292-9129
Email: dbswashingtondc@gmail.com

We are excited to have you join us and be a part of our spiritual journey!

BOOK SHELF

Taking the Church Beyond the Walls is a testimony of how Destiny Church for All Nations (London), under the leadership of Pastor Adebo, has succeeded in converting the revelation of the gospel of the Kingdom, as taught by pastor Sunday Adelaja, into visible and tangible results. It is full of practical wisdom and ideas that can inspire readers to become more relevant in their communities.

The Role of the Supernatural is a follow-up to Taking the Church Beyond the Walls, the documented testimony of how Destiny Church for all Nations, London, under the leadership of Pastor Adebo & Hyelazira Tomomewo began to reach out to the homeless in the heart of London. It shows the important role the Holy Spirit in converting the gospel of the Kingdom into visible and tangible result. Full practical wisdom to become more relevant in their respective communities.

Power of Communion for Total Health. In this book, I am introducing to you the Holy Communion as the balm in Gilead ordained for the recovery of your total health. This is the physician's prescription for our health.
When you take the Holy Communion, you may not experience the spectacular but you will experience the supernatural. You may not experience some spectacular physical manifestation like something happening to you e.g. shaking or trembling, but you will experience the supernatural operations in your health and you add years to your life.

Born With a Destiny. Your destiny is a journey. Every day you are either walking within your destiny or walking away from it. Destiny is what everybody is born with but is coded. It is your birth right to decode your destiny that is veiled in a mystery or hidden away and, once found, fulfil it with God's help. When you are born with a destiny it means you are born with a purpose. This book will teach you how to find, follow and fulfil it.

You Will Not End the Journey Half Way (DVD). This teaching series primarily addresses why fail to achieve their vision. Through divine revelation of Gods word, Pastor Adebo Tomomewo uncovers the true reasons why people fail to accomplish their God given vision. This teaching covers:
- Why people finish halfway
- Understanding the place of vision
- Prophetic words for finishing strong
- 5 things you inherit through the Abrahamic covenant.

Why Do Bad Things Happen To Good People? The foremost reason why bad things happen to good people is ignorance. The Devil's greater weapon is ignorance. You can fight a battle you don't know exist.

In this teaching, the Lord will send His light into the dark areas of your life and expose the hidden sources of your troubles. This book will show you:
- How to discern between clean and unclean
- Blocking Satan's legal ground to your life
- Recognizing accursed things as sources of hidden trouble
- Confronting the Devils in your bloodline 1&2

Operating In Deliverance. This book is written to enlighten God's people that deliverance is a ministry of every blood-bought child of God on the earth. The Bible says the signs shall follow them that believe; it is not a ministry reserved for those in the five-fold ministry only, every believer can operate in deliverance. This book will teach you the biblical basis for deliverance and how to walk in the anointing that brings deliverance to the captives. You are meant to be a deliverer to your generation. The world is waiting for you.

Master Key To Freedom. The focus of this book will be on how to take the right steps to freedom as a believer. You must know there is a difference between deliverance and freedom. Your deliverance was effected on the platform of redemption by the blood of Jesus Christ. which is free, but freedom is not free. And I wrote this book to teach you on how to lay hold on the master key of freedom, and I trust God that the master key to freedom shall be delivered into your hand before you finish reading this book.

The Truth Satan Does Not Want You To Know. Though we are all living many of us do not know the true meaning of life. As an individual it is important to understand that life is a possession to treasure. If you lose life, you lose everything. If you carry out a survey and ask people about the meaning of life, the definition on life will not be the same for everyone.

63 Scriptural Facts About Wisdom. This book emphasizes the paramount importance of wisdom as highlighted in the Bible. The author, inspired by biblical references, undertakes an extensive study on wisdom, noting its crucial role in both the creation process and in Jesus' life and ministry. The book suggests that if wisdom was essential for divine beings, its significance for humans is even greater. Readers are encouraged to seek an increase in wisdom through the insights offered in the book.

Help Me! I Want to Be Married and Stay Married. This book explores the concept that marriage is about completion, not competition. Reflecting on his 25-year marital journey, the author shares insights for singles aspiring to marry and for those already married to maintain their union. Emphasizing that marriage is a God-ordained institution, the book aims to enlighten, educate, and empower readers for marital success, highlighting the importance of marrying according to God's purpose and providing practical knowledge for a successful marital journey.

Making Right Choices is a book aimed at assisting individuals dealing with substance misuse issues, often stemming from poor decision-making. Additionally, it delves into the impact of illegal drugs on children's brain development. The book is designed to provide readers with information and guidance to make healthier choices in their life pursuits, focusing on overcoming substance-related challenges and fostering better decision-making skills.

Last Minute Miracle. This book offers an insightful perspective that miracles are the outcomes of a process rather than random events. Addressing various life challenges, it encourages active engagement in this process, emphasizing empowerment and divine intervention as key to overcoming life's obstacles. The key message of "Last Minute Miracles" is empowerment through understanding. It encourages readers to not just passively wait for miracles but to actively engage in the process that leads to them.

Wisdom For Family Peace.

This book underscores the idea that life's challenges, particularly in family and finances, are essentially wisdom problems. It posits that peace in family life stems from the application of divine wisdom, asserting that a lack of peace indicates a deficiency in wisdom. This book provides straightforward wisdom keys to help readers achieve harmony in their family relationships.

Your Faith Will Not Fail.

This book is written by a pastor drawing from his counseling experiences, emphasizing that life's challenges often stem from misapplied faith. The book advocates for an active, contending approach to faith, rather than a passive one, presenting it as a vital tool to overcome life's inherent unfairness. Inspired by the way the pandemic has tested faith, the author aims to ignite a revival in the reader's heart, strengthening their faith and resilience.

All books are available on Amazon.

The picture here shows our impact in the community, you see our members reaching out to the elderly during Christmas, testimonies of transformation being shared by those that attend the breakfast service on one of pastor Adebo outings. Tuesday personal development discipleship class with Sis. Anna Atu and the table set for their dinner, pupils of supplementary school at the inaugural day of the school In April 2009.

Support Logo given us in acknowledgment of community impact, by Southwark borough council of London England.

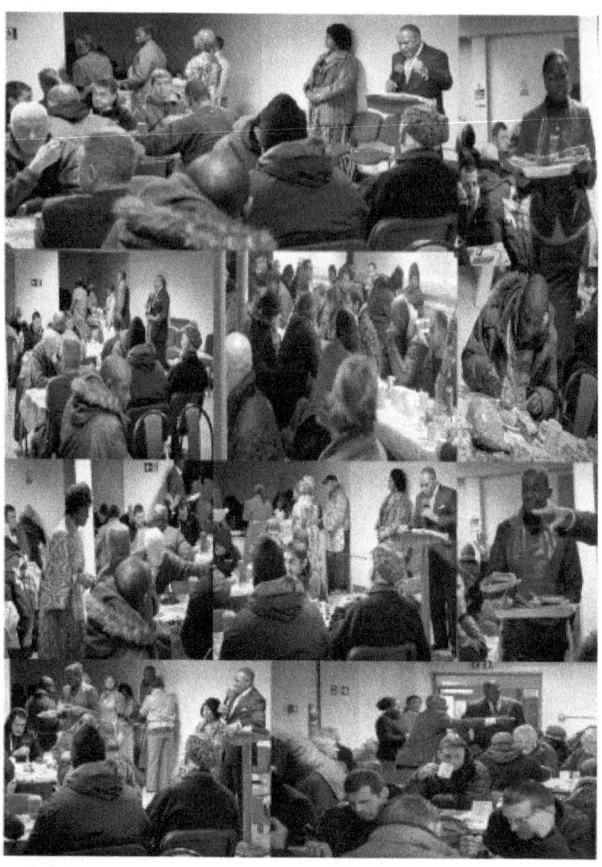

This picture show the first service of the Destiny Church, London, our kitchen runs, called Jesus breakfast service that started with 10 people from the streets of London been served full English breakfast, it has grown to become our first service today, within the auditorium we seen 200 people, this breakfast takes place every Sunday 9:00 am to the homeless, rough sleepers and the hungry. Over 1000 homeless have visited our feeding project every Sunday in the city of London. Come and see lives of people being radically changed as they hear the gospel of the Kingdom while eating their breakfast.

1. Dr. Adebo at History makers training in Kiev Ukraine
2. Dr. Adebo after a ministration in Vienna Austria
3. Dr. Adebo after ministering in Kiev Ukraine

1. Dr. Adebo, when invited to the house of commons, July 2011; 2. Dr. Adebo with Governor Olusegun Agagu, Ondo state in Akure Nigeria, 2006.; 3. Dr. Adebo with Former Nigerian Head of state, General Yakubu Gowon.; 4. Dr. Adebo in Downing street, poising for a snap shot with other delegates at the prime minister door, Whitehall London England.; 5. Dr. Adebo with Former Mayor of London, Ken Livingstone, 2010; 6. Dr. Adebo with the present Mayor Boris Johnson 2011; 7. Dr. Adebo with Valerie Shawcross. London Assembly member for the borough Lambeth and Southwark.; (This pictures explain the chapter that deals with the church with influence)

1. Dr. Adebo with pastor Sunday Adelaja and Apostle Alfred Williams; 2. Dr. Adebo with pastor W.F. Kumuyi and his wife; 3. Pastor Adebo with pastor Mike Tomomewo at the edge; 4. Dr. Adebo with pastor Natalya Potopayeva in Frankfurt Germany; 5. Dr. Adebo with Apostle Tuff and his wife; 6. Dr. Adebo, Bishop Jide Orire, pastor (Mrs) Stella and others; 7. Dr. Adebo and pastor Andy hawthorn of The message Trust at house of commons; 8. Dr. Adebo with bishop Wayne Malcolm at house of commons; 9. Dr. Adebo, Bishop Nelson, Dr. Agbeyomi from Altanta USA, Late Mayor Tayo Situ and wife.

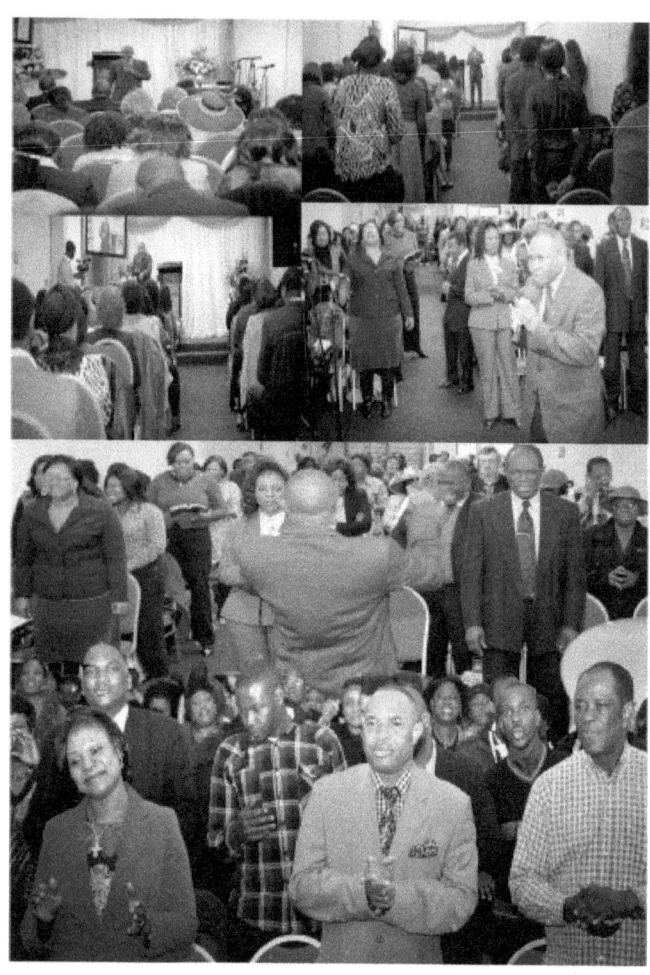

This picture show the first service of the Destiny Chiurch, London, our kitchen runs, called Jesus breakfast service that started with 10 people from the street of London been served full English breakfast, it has grown to become our first service today, with - in the auditorium we seen 200 people, this breakfast take place every Sunday 9:00am to the homeless, rough sleepers and the hungry, over 1000 homeless has visited our feeding project every Sunday in the city of London. Come and see lives of people being radically changed as they hear the gospel of the kingdom while eating their breakfast.

Destiny Church, Washington. D.C.
Church Sunday services.

Feeding ministry for the homeless and for those having substance misuse issues.

July 2nd, 2018. Dr. Adebo and his wife, pastor (Mrs) Hyelazira Tomomewo, along with three children David, Elijah and Princess at graduation ceremony. Arts foundation degree in drugs & alcohol treatment and counseling, University of Leicester.

Dr. Adebo on the invitation to the US Senate as participant on the national day of prayer.

SENATOR MIKE BROWN & U.S REPRESENTATIVE CONGRESS OYE ADDRESS THE CHURCH DURING SUNDAY SERVICE AND DISTRIBUTE TURKEY TO THOSE IN THE NEIGHBOURHOOD IN WASHINGTON D.C.

STEVEN HORSFORD, CONGRESSMAN FOR NEVADA, CHAIRMAN OF THE CONGRESSIONAL BLACK COCCUS ACROSS U.S.A.

This is the certificate of recognition from U.S Senator and congressmen in the U.S Congress representing Las Vegas for our work in the community

DESTINY CHURCH FOR ALL NATIONS WASHINGTONDC USA

5209, GEORGIA AVENUE NW WASHINGTON D.C. 20111

www.ingramcontent.com/pod-product-compliance
Lightning Source LLC
Chambersburg PA
CBHW031137090426
42738CB00008B/1122